Following
THE
Path OF THE
Eagle

DAVID O. OYEDEPO

FOLLOWING THE PATH OF THE EAGLE

© 2017 by David O. Oyedepo

ISBN 978 – 2480 – 24

Published in Nigeria by:

DOMINION PUBLISHING HOUSE

All rights reserved.

For further information or permission, address:

DOMINION PUBLISHING HOUSE

Km 10, Idiroko Road, Canaan Land, Ota, Nigeria.

Tel: +234 816 406 0777, +234 909 151 4022

Or visit our website: ***www.dphprints.com***

Connect with David O. Oyedepo

 @davidoyedepomin   *davidoyedepomin*

 faithtabernacle.org.ng   *David Oyedepo Ministries International*

All Scripture quotations are from the King James Version of the Bible, except otherwise stated.

CONTENT

Introduction

We understand from the Scripture that every child of God is redeemed as a spiritual eagle and, therefore, ordained to scale unimaginable heights in life. However, just like an eagle goes through different stages of growth, we must go through processes for the eagle in us to attain the heights specially prepared by God.

The eagle symbolises greatness! Unlike other birds, it is capable of mounting up to unbelievable heights, far above the mountains. While most birds go to hide when there is a storm, the eagle delights in the stormy winds, accompanied by lightning and thunder. In fact, the eagle rides on the storm, using air currents, which destroy things on the ground, to carry itself to heights invisible to the human eye. Contrary to expectation, the eagle does not flap its wings to fly or struggle against the storm. Rather, it locks its wings, picks the air thermals, thrusts upward and rides on it. It locks its wings to ensure that nothing deters its upward thrusts, and then it soars!

However, the eagle, which fears nothing and to whom great storms are play things, was not born fearless. It was born an eaglet – weak, fearful and totally dependent on its mother. The ability to be fearless and soar to great heights was in the eaglet, but it took special trainings from the mother-eagle to make an eagle out of the eaglet. From Deuteronomy 32:9-14, we discover that the Lord led Israel through the wilderness to bring him to the land flowing with milk and honey. This can be likened to how the mother-eagle trains her young ones.

As we all know, a finished product is always a thing of joy to behold. For instance, a finished piece of pottery stands out in beauty; and a fanciful building block is the joy of a builder. These, however, did not fall from heaven; they all had a beginning. They were all raw materials at one point in time that underwent processes, which resulted in their present glorious shapes. In the same vein, we are raw materials which God moulds (if allowed) into His desired shapes. However, God has given man the right to choose whether to undergo the difficult shaping processes or remain a raw material liable to decay.

The making of a man is in his hands; that is, he must be determined to go through the making processes by himself, not on another person's back. That is why the Bible says:

Know ye not that they which run in a race run all,
but one receiveth the prize? So run, that ye may
obtain. And every man that striveth for the mastery
is temperate in all things. Now they do it to obtain
a corruptible crown; but we an incorruptible. I
therefore so run, not as uncertainly; so fight I, not
as one that beateth the air.

1 Corinthians 9:24-26

It is impossible to become a star using another man's feet, because it is the personal exercises we engage in that determine our efficiency on the racetrack.

Children are born while men are made. Being born again does not make us automatically great. We must work our way up the ladder. God is ready to lead, instruct and bless us but we must "do the climbing". For instance, even though eagles are born to soar, they are trained to soar. Training is a lifelong responsibility of every sportsman, if he must remain relevant. Likewise, taking personal responsibility is a daily requirement for any believer to fulfil God's plan and purpose for his/her life.

The purpose of this book, among others, is to unveil the worth of our destinies in Christ, examine the characteristics of the eagle which helps it to scale great heights and to show how to apply same to our lives as believers, thereby fulfilling our glorious destinies, and soaring like the eagle. As you read this book, God will set your feet on the path of greatness, in Jesus' name! Remain ever blessed!

1

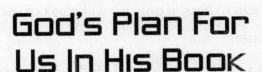

God's Plan For
Us In His Book

*For I know the thoughts that I think toward you,
saith the LORD, thoughts of peace, and not of evil,
to give you an expected end.*

Jeremiah 29:11

The Bible, as a book of visions, shows us who we are in Christ, what we are worth in redemption, what we can do and how to do them. However, it is important to recognise that every plan of God is a covenant. The covenant unveils His plans and also spells out our responsibilities in actualising them. If we are not interested or committed to our part, the covenant will remain a mere religious theory as nothing may come out of it.

Since April 1977, when God spoke to me from Jeremiah 29:11 that, your future is in My plan, not in your plan, I have been craving God's plan at every stage of my life.

Isaiah 14:24 says:

*The LORD of hosts hath sworn, saying, Surely as I
have thought, so shall it come to pass; and as I have
purposed, so shall it stand.*

God has plans for us and has bound Himself with an oath
to bring them to pass, if only we will play our own part.

It is written:

*But be ye doers of the word, and not hearers only,
deceiving your own selves.*
*For if any be a hearer of the word, and not a doer, he is
like unto a man beholding his natural face in a glass:*
*For he beholdeth himself, and goeth his way, and
straightway forgetteth what manner of man he was.*
*But whoso looketh into the perfect law of liberty,
and continueth therein, he being not a forgetful
hearer, but a doer of the work, this man shall be
blessed in his deed.*

James 1:22-25

From the above scripture, we understand that God's
visions for His people are contained in His Book which
is the spiritual mirror that reveals the actual worth
of the redeemed. Therefore, as we discover our worth
from the Word, and accept the responsibility it places
on us, it becomes a reality. It was said about Jesus, **"In
the volume of the book it is written of me."** Similarly,
there are things written about us in the volume of the

Book (the Bible) which we need to discover.

It is important to recognise, however, that the discovery of God's plans for our lives begins with new birth. That is, until we are born again, we can never access God's plans from the Bible, because only the redeemed are qualified *to know the mystery of the kingdom of God* (Mark 4:11).

Moreover, every unsaved soul cannot access the rhema in the Word but believers can. As it is written:

> *And the vision of all is become unto you as the words of a book that is sealed, which men deliver to one that is learned, saying, Read this, I pray thee: and he saith, I cannot; for it is sealed: And the book is delivered to him that is not learned, saying, Read this, I pray thee: and he saith, I am not learned.*
>
> *Isaiah 29:11-12*

We must also understand that, by redemption, our lives are ordained to shine brighter and brighter. For the Bible says: *But the path of the just is as the shining light, that shineth more and more unto the perfect day* (Proverbs 4:18). Therefore, we are redeemed to enjoy a 'from glory to glory' lifestyle. As it is written:

> *But we all, with open face beholding as in a glass the glory of the Lord, are changed into the same image from glory to glory, even as by the Spirit of the Lord.*
>
> *2 Corinthians 3:18*

Our lives should be characterised by beauty and colour because we are redeemed to enjoy breakthroughs not breakdowns. Again, we understand from the Scripture that we are the salt of the earth, the light of the world and cities set on hills that cannot be hidden. Therefore, whatever is pushing you into obscurity ends now! I command whatever is pressing you down in any area of your life to take its hands off you right now, in the name of Jesus!

In 1970, I discovered from the Bible that God's plan for man is to access his glorious future through high-level discipline. It is written: *It is good for a man that he bear the yoke in his youth* (Lamentations 3:27). Thereafter, I went behind the dormitory, knelt down and said, "Jesus, any yoke that I will need to bear when I am old, let me bear it now." That was how much I understood it then.

Today, by that revelation, there are no struggles in my life; I command results at the instance of light. Therefore, we are empowered for change of levels only by revelation. As it is written:

Arise, shine; for thy light is come, and the glory of the LORD is risen upon thee.
For, behold, the darkness shall cover the earth, and gross darkness the people: but the LORD shall arise

upon thee, and his glory shall be seen upon thee.

And the Gentiles shall come to thy light, and kings to the brightness of thy rising.

Who are these that fly as a cloud, and as the doves to their windows?

A little one shall become a thousand, and a small one a strong nation: I the LORD will hasten it in his time.

Isaiah 60:1-3, 8, 22

Also, in 1970, I discovered from Revelation 5:10 that we have been redeemed unto our God as priests and kings and ordained to reign on earth. Instantly, I concluded that I am not redeemed a peasant, struggler or beggar; rather, I am redeemed into royalty. By that revelation, at the age of 16, I would ask myself when going out whether a king would go out dressed that way. If the answer was "no", I would go back home to change. I saw that I am redeemed to be a king; so, I must not walk about as a slave.

In addition, I was the Secretary of a Disciplinary Committee headed by my Principal. By the light of Scripture, I have been dining with kings for long. Likewise, I discovered from the Scripture that kings don't strive, because they are not troublemakers, but lovers of peace. In essence, catching our picture from the Bible definitely creates our future. However, we must understand that it is not what we know that changes our position but what we do with what we know. It is written:

> *And it shall come to pass, if thou shalt hearken diligently unto the voice of the LORD thy God, to observe and to do all his commandments which I command thee this day, that the LORD thy God will set thee on high above all nations of the earth.*
>
> Deuteronomy 28:1

Therefore, it is not enough to capture God's picture of our future from His Word, we must be committed to walking in it. Many years ago, the Lord said to me, **Seest thou a man diligent in his business? he shall stand before kings; he shall not stand before mean men** (Proverbs 22:29).

By that light, it has become my delight and addiction to put my best into every assignment. Since the Bible is a Book of covenants that demands responsibilities from the believer, any faith that seeks to make God absolutely responsible for the outcome of our lives is an irresponsible faith. Thus, we must not watch our lives grounded. Our Church (Living Faith Church Worldwide) came out of stagnation after we fasted for three days. Also, I got my tongue touched with a coal of fire after waiting on the Lord in a fast for three days. I wonder why people play with their lives as if they have a spare.

The truth is, it takes strange works to experience

strange acts. If we won't do what is strange, we will never be entitled to strange manifestations of God. Understand that God is not a joker; He says what He means and means what He says. Therefore, we must endeavour to do whatever He tells us to do. It is also important to recognise that despite the fact that our needs are genuine, until we obey what God commands, they will never be met.

In 1981, the Lord said to me, "You are absolutely responsible for the outcome of your life, with no one to blame." Thereafter, I took practical and absolute responsibility for the outcome of my life.

There is a testimony of a woman in Santa, Texas, whose baby, while in the womb, was certified deformed as a result of a disease that made the head of the child bigger than usual. There was fluid in the baby's brain; part of the brain was missing and the doctors said that if the child ever lived, he would never be normal. However, this daughter of Abraham took responsibility when she heard that God still works miracles through praise. With the advanced pregnancy, she engaged in wild praise and the baby was born perfect. Science was proved wrong!

God cannot praise for us; He has told us what our testimony requires. We have to praise Him before He can intervene in our affairs. It is all about responsibility. For instance, if you are praying for financial breakthrough and you are not a "tither", your breakthrough is not in view. This is because we cannot get to God on our terms, but on His.

Years ago, Kenneth E. Hagin told a story of a cub that was captured and raised among sheep. Each time they went to the river to drink water and sighted a lion on the other side, the sheep, including the 'lion-sheep', took to their heels for safety. One day, the 'lion-sheep' discovered its identity through its reflection in the water. There, he saw that he didn't look like the sheep but like the lion they had been running away from. As a result, the next time a lion appeared and the other sheep ran away, he escaped to join his family. By reason of the revelation from the Bible, you are crossing to the victory side, in the name of Jesus Christ!

On September 12, 1976, God delivered to me the master key of life from Matthew 6:33. He said, *Seek ye first My Kingdom and all its demands and all these things that others are dying to get shall be added unto you.* That day, I entered into a covenant to take responsibility by making Kingdom stewardship my lifestyle. Today, nothing turns me on like the matters of the Kingdom. In essence, it has become my only focus and it is exciting, fulfilling and enriching.

I preached my first message in 1970 and started

preaching in crusades at 21. I was 'crusading' the devil out of people's lives although I had no idea I would be called into ministry. I was just an addict of God's Kingdom because I entered into a covenant with Him. God will appear to you through His book (the Bible) and all you need is to position yourself to qualify for His appearance.

It is written:

> *But the natural man receiveth not the things of the Spirit of God: for they are foolishness unto him: neither can he know them, because they are spiritually discerned.*
>
> *1 Corinthians 2:14*

On March 1, 1992, God showed up and said, "Woe unto you when all men shall speak good of you, for so they did to their fathers the first prophets." Then the Spirit of God came upon me and I began to write a poem. Surprisingly, as soon as I finished, a woman came in to apologise for the evil things she had said about me. I smiled because God spoke to me before she came and I forgave her instantly from the depth of my heart.

One day, my wife said that she heard that someone was saying some things about me on a television programme. I responded, "Can a person go on television and be quiet? He has to say something." Amazingly, as the attack became more severe, the church was growing stronger. That attack was part of the catalyst that brought us to Canaanland because within a year, Church attendance became 10,000; which was an increase of 7,000. Within 10 years of being in Lagos, our church grew to 50,000 worshippers! That is the power of revelation. Get set, because God will show us who we are from His Book and that will make all the difference in our lives forever.

2

Our Pictures in Redemption

For whom he did foreknow, he also did predestinate to be conformed to the image of his Son, that he might be the firstborn among many brethren.

Moreover whom he did predestinate, them he also called: and whom he called, them he also justified: and whom he justified, them he also glorified.

Romans 8:29-30

Through redemption, we have become joint-heirs with Christ. We are redeemed to share same DNA with Christ, thereby sharing the same nature, potential and capacity with Him. Therefore, the end product of our predestination is glorification.

However, no one ever arrives at a future he cannot see. We must see it first before we can ever get there; that is, we must catch a vision and have a revelation from the

Scripture. For instance, Abraham saw his future before he could get there. The Bible records:

> *And the LORD said unto Abram, after that Lot was separated from him, Lift up now thine eyes, and look from the place where thou art northward, and southward, and eastward, and westward: For all the land which thou seest, to thee will I give it, and to thy seed for ever. And I will make thy seed as the dust of the earth: so that if a man can number the dust of the earth, then shall thy seed also be numbered. Arise, walk through the land in the length of it and in the breadth of it; for I will give it unto thee.*
>
> *Genesis 13:14-17*

We must also understand that we are redeemed for greatness, not mediocrity. This is because we have mountaintop destinies in redemption and we are cities set on hills that cannot be hidden.

Even when I was not married, I was too sure of a hitch-free marriage because the terms were clearly spelt out. In March 1984, the terms of church growth were also spelt out and I dived into them. In addition, the terms of supernatural prosperity were spelt out and I committed myself to them wholeheartedly. God said to me, "My son, David, my prosperity plan is not a promise, so it does not answer to prayer; it's not a promise, it has no respect for fasting. My prosperity plan is a covenant and until your part is played, I am not committed."

Every destiny is at the mercy of obedience. That is, our future places specific demands on our lives that we must subscribe to.

Therefore, until we profess obedience, our confession is fake because we cannot confuse God with our confession. Remember, He is smarter than all of us. Thus, confession without profession equals confusion. The Bible says: *In all labour there is profit: but the talk of the lips tendeth only to penury* (Proverbs 14:23).

Let's See Some Very Clear Pictures of Who we are in Redemption

Every Child of God is Redeemed to Walk in Dominion

> *...Be fruitful, and multiply, and replenish the earth, and subdue it: and have dominion over the fish of the sea, and over the fowl of the air, and over every living thing that moveth upon the earth.*
>
> *Genesis 1:28*

"Dominion" simply means, being on top of life's situations and circumstances. We are created in God's image and in His very likeness to command dominion after the order of divinity. From the Scripture, we see that by redemption, we are seated with Christ in heavenly places far above the forces tormenting and making life miserable for others. The Bible says:

> *Surely there is no enchantment against Jacob, neither is there any divination against Israel: according to this time it shall be said of Jacob and of Israel, What hath God wrought!*
>
> *Numbers 23:23*

Redemption has repositioned us for 'sweatless' triumph and we are to **tread upon serpents and scorpions, and over all the powers of the enemy and nothing shall by any means hurt us** (Luke 10:19).

It is also written: **And hath raised us up together, and made us sit together in heavenly places in Christ Jesus** (Ephesians 2:6).

In other words, we are seated with Jesus, far above where witches celebrate triumph as they afflict and make bold speeches. By this repositioning, we are placed far above the oppression of occult powers and generational curses. We need to carry this 'far above' mentality.

For instance, since 1979, I have been conscious that no agent of the devil under the sun can stand on my path, and that no witch in the world can withstand me. Not that I prayed; I knew and I shouted it everywhere! Remember the Bible says: **And ye shall know the truth, and the truth shall make you free** (John 8:32).

We stepped into Liberia in 2009 and the Queen of

Sheba had no choice but to step out. Witches know that there are people they can't resist. There is no mad person that does not know fire. We have been translated far above every force behind all barriers – both visible and invisible.

However, revelation is the master key to walking in dominion because the dominion of light over darkness is eternally unquestionable.

> **And the light shineth in darkness; and the darkness comprehended it not.**
>
> John 1:5

We must, therefore, understand that there is no barrier before us that can challenge the authority of the revelation of the truth that we believe. This is because we are empowered to become whatever we believe (Ephesians 2:5-6, 1:20-21; John 1:12).

Moreover, at salvation, we become supernatural beings. The Bible says:

> **Behold, I and the children whom the LORD hath given me are for signs and for wonders in Israel from the LORD of hosts, which dwelleth in mount Zion.**
>
> Isaiah 8:18 (see also John 3:8)

When we become born again, we are raised and made to sit together with Christ in heavenly places, far above all principalities and powers (Ephesians 1:20-21, 2:5-6).

Remember,

> *...whatsoever is born of God overcometh the world: and this is the victory that overcometh the world, even our faith.*

1 John 5:4

We are Ordained to be the Salt of the Earth and the Light of the World

Salt is an essential commodity of universal and global relevance. It is known to be a preservative; and it is very essential to the taste of any meal. Therefore, we are redeemed and ordained to be positive influences in terms of preservation, restoration and taste. It is important to recognise that we are not permitted to experience salvation alone. This is because by redemption, we and our household are ordained to be saved. When the prison gates were flung open through Paul and Silas' praise, the jailer said:

> *...Sirs, what must I do to be saved? And they said, Believe on the Lord Jesus Christ, and thou shalt be saved, <u>and thy house</u>.*

Acts 16:30-31

Therefore, redemption does not only guarantee our escape but that of our household. Thus, your salvation must not end with you; your household must also be saved. The Bible says:

> *And saviours shall come up on mount Zion to judge the mount of Esau; and the kingdom shall be the LORD's.*
>
> *Obadiah 1:21*

We are saved to ensure the salvation of other members of our household. For instance, Joseph was saved to become the saviour of his father, his brethren and ultimately, his generation.

As the light of the world, we are also ordained to lead and be the envy of our world (Matthew 5:13-14). That means we are redeemed as pacesetters and trailblazers, to be relevant to our generation. We are to show the world the way and set a standard for doing things.

We are Redeemed as Kings to Reign on Earth

> *And they sung a new song, saying, Thou art worthy to take the book, and to open the seals thereof: for thou wast slain, and hast redeemed us to God by thy blood out of every kindred, and tongue, and people, and nation;*
> *And hast made us unto our God kings and priests: and we shall reign on the earth.*
>
> *Revelation 5:9-10 (see also Isaiah 62:3)*

From the above scripture, we see that we have been redeemed as kings and priests to reign on the earth. Hence, we have royal destinies. Our enthronement is not a function of our colour. God is neither black nor white; God is God! Thus far, we have been intimidated to live as destitute Christians, but that must end now. We must recognise that we have a universal gospel that delivers at the same rate in every nation, among every tribe, tongue and race.

The Bible says we have been redeemed as peculiar people, royal priesthoods and holy nations to live marvellous lives, for Jesus came to give us life in abundance. He came to take us off the realm of struggles to the realm of miracles. Therefore, our case is different. We must also understand that redemption has made us not just spiritual Jews, but members of the ever-winning, ever-conquering and ever-reigning tribe of Judah.

Judah, thou art he whom thy brethren shall praise: thy hand shall be in the neck of thine enemies; thy father's children shall bow down before thee. Judah is a lion's whelp: from the prey, my son, thou art gone up: he stooped down, he couched as a lion, and as an old lion; who shall rouse him up? The sceptre shall not depart from Judah, nor a lawgiver from between his feet, until Shiloh come; and unto him shall the gathering of the people be. Binding his foal unto the vine, and his ass's colt unto the choice vine; he washed his garments in wine, and his clothes in the blood of grapes. His eyes shall be

red with wine, and his teeth white with milk.
Genesis 49:8-12

Judah is never to be pitied but to be praised! Therefore, every area of pity in our lives is turned to envy, in the name of Jesus!

We are Redeemed as Stars to Shine!

I Jesus have sent mine angel to testify unto you these things in the churches. I am the root and the offspring of David, and the bright and morning star.
Revelation 22:16

Jesus further said: *As thou hast sent me into the world, even so have I also sent them into the world.*
John 17:18

Therefore, every child of God is redeemed a star after the order of Christ. We may look like charcoal now, but we are stars in the making.

Every star today was like charcoal yesterday but as he continued to engage in the required exercises, the star in him began to surface little by little until he came out full blown. We are potential stars because we are redeemed for the topmost top. "A star" connotes being the best among equals in career, business and ministry. Being a star means to be a pathfinder, a pacesetter and a trailblazer. A star is someone at the top of his field of endeavour.

Being born again means to be born a star, but that is unrealisable except by the Spirit of God. The Bible, with reference to Philip, says, "The Spirit of the Lord caught away Philip" (Acts 8:39).

But, what does it take for our stars to shine?

And they that be wise shall shine as the brightness of the firmament; and they that turn many to righteousness as the stars for ever and ever.

Daniel 12:3

It is also written:

The fruit of the righteous is a tree of life; and he that winneth souls is wise.

Proverbs 11:30

If turning many to righteousness is winning souls for the Kingdom and he that wins souls is wise, that means, turning many to righteousness is one of the mysteries for the making of stars in the Kingdom.

Moreover, when we are 'on the go' for Christ, interceding for the Kingdom in prayers and reaching out to the lost with passion and love, we are in partnership with Christ.

Jesus came primarily to save souls; His miracles only validated that He is the Messiah. So, if we are not concerned about the core interest of Jesus, how can we walk with Him? What is His core interest? God does not want anyone to perish but that all should come to the knowledge of the Saviour (1 Timothy 2:4; 2 Peter 3:9). Therefore, our star may never shine without us being passionate about the things of the Kingdom!

We are Redeemed to be Givers, not Beggars

For ye know the grace of our Lord Jesus Christ, that, though he was rich, yet for your sakes he became poor, that ye through his poverty might be rich.
2 Corinthians 8:9 (see also John 10:10)

We must recognise that we are redeemed into a wealthy place; therefore, we cannot afford to be beggars. Remember, heaven is the epitome of wealth. As it is written:

And the building of the wall of it was of jasper: and the city was pure gold, like unto clear glass. And the foundations of the wall of the city were garnished with all manner of precious stones. The first foundation was jasper; the second, sapphire; the third, a chalcedony; the fourth, an emerald;

The fifth, sardonyx; the sixth, sardius; the seventh, chrysolite; the eighth, beryl; the ninth, a topaz; the tenth, a chrysoprasus; the eleventh, a jacinth; the twelfth, an amethyst. And the twelve gates were twelve pearls; every several gate was of one pearl: and the street of the city was pure gold, as it were transparent glass.
Revelation 21:18-21

From that scripture, we understand that the walls in heaven are built with precious stones and all the buildings are made of pure gold. Also, precious stones were used for the foundation of the city. That is the picture of heaven where we are seated.

We are Redeemed to be Fruitful Vines not Barren Figs

Blessed is every one that feareth the LORD; that walketh in his ways.

For thou shalt eat the labour of thine hands: happy shalt thou be, and it shall be well with thee. Thy wife shall be as a fruitful vine by the sides of thine house: thy children like olive plants round about thy table. Behold, that thus shall the man be blessed that feareth the LORD. The LORD shall bless thee out of Zion: and thou shalt see the good of Jerusalem all the days of thy life. Yea, thou shalt see thy children's children, and peace upon Israel.

Psalm 128:1-5 (see also Isaiah 5:1-13)

We must recognise that we are redeemed fruitful vines because every child of God is a branch of Jesus, the Vine. Jesus said:

I am the vine, ye are the branches: He that abideth in me, and I in him, the same bringeth forth much fruit: for without me ye can do nothing.

John 15:5

As long as the Vine is fruitful, the branches must be fruitful. There is no day without many people coming into the Kingdom. Therefore, we cannot be listed among the barren.

It is people who call those who have not been blessed with the fruit of womb 'barren'. Concerning Elizabeth, the Bible records that, "It is six months with her who was called barren." People called her barren and she accepted it. Therefore, she remained barren until God stepped in and said, "No, it is not I who called you that; people called you so!" Every negative name people may have called you in the hospital, the neighbourhood or in your home is hereby reversed, in Jesus' name!

Thy wife shall be as a fruitful vine by the sides of thine house: thy children like olive plants round about thy table.

Psalm 128:3

We are redeemed as fruitful vines; therefore, barrenness is not our portion. Thus, we have children already. In fact, the Bible says, we shall teach these things to our children and children's children. That is, we have the assignment of teaching them. This also means that our children are right inside us because God cannot send us on an impossible or unaccomplishable mission. He can't tell us that our children will be around our tables and we would teach them certain things if that has not been established. He is not trying to entertain us but to show us who we are.

It is important to understand that the misfortune in our biological families is no longer our portion because our family lineage changed at redemption. Among the things that became new at redemption are: our family tree and root. We were once sons (children) of men but now, we are sons and daughters of God, which makes us members of God's family. Since we cannot belong to two families at the same time, it means an eternal change took place at new birth. Therefore, anything negative associated with us in our biological lineage no longer holds because we don't belong to that natural order any more.

Moreover, we were like wild olive trees now grafted into the good olive trees, thereby becoming partakers of its fatness. Thus, whatever obtains in the past is no longer our portion because there is already a disconnection. This clearly defines what took place at new birth. We need this understanding; otherwise, we will continue to partake of the woes and calamities of the old tree (Romans 11:17-24).

Therefore, fruitfulness is our heritage in Christ because we belong to a fruitful vine!

At creation, God initiated a covenant of fruitfulness with man when He said:

> *...Be fruitful, and multiply, and replenish the earth, and subdue it: and have dominion over the fish of the sea, and over the fowl of the air, and over every living thing that moveth upon the earth.*
>
> *Genesis 1:28*

Immediately those words were uttered, everything man needed to make him fruitful was deposited in him. What God said at the beginning is still in force today and nothing can tamper with it.

We Are Redeemed to be Greater than all the Old Testament Saints

> *Verily I say unto you, Among them that are born of women there hath not risen a greater than John the Baptist: notwithstanding he that is least in the kingdom of heaven is greater than he.*
>
> *Matthew 11:11*

Speaking about Himself, Jesus said, "A greater-than-Solomon is here," and as the Father has sent Him, so has He sent us. That means inside every believer is a greater-than-Solomon potential (Matthew 12:42; John 17:18).

However, it is one thing to have potentials, and another to realise it. For instance, John the Baptist was greater than Elijah, Isaac, Jacob and other Old Testament saints; yet, he died cheaply because he did not realise it. You will realise your potentials and fulfil destiny, in Jesus' name!

We are Redeemed as Lively Stones to Enjoy Health and Vitality

Ye also, as lively stones, are built up a spiritual house, an holy priesthood, to offer up spiritual sacrifices, acceptable to God by Jesus Christ.

1 Peter 2:5

By redemption, we share eternal life with God and that in turn guarantees our immunity from all sicknesses and diseases.

Surely he hath borne our griefs, and carried our sorrows: yet we did esteem him stricken, smitten of God, and afflicted. But he was wounded for our transgressions, he was bruised for our iniquities: the chastisement of our peace was upon him; and with his stripes we are healed.

Isaiah 53:4-5 (see also 1 Peter 2:24)

Healthy living is a core aspect of our redemption. That is one area where the devil oppresses humanity the most. Sickness, which is an oppression of the devil, is never from God. The Bible says that Jesus went about doing good and healing them that were oppressed of the devil. No sane parent will poison his/her children, no matter how disobedient they are. In the same vein, God will not give poison to His children because sickness is poison to our bodies. It is written:

> *When the even was come, they brought unto him many that were possessed with devils: and he cast out the spirits with his word, and healed all that were sick: That it might be fulfilled which was spoken by Esaias the prophet, saying, Himself took our infirmities, and bare our sicknesses.*
>
> *Matthew 8:16-17*

From the scripture above, "grief" means infirmities or sicknesses and "infirmities" connote disabilities, discomforts or diseases. Therefore, whatever is contrary to our ease is a disease. We must understand that Jesus is not just the Saviour of our soul but also of our body. Concerning the journey of the Israelites in the wilderness, the Bible records: *He brought them forth also with silver and gold: and there was not one feeble person among their tribes* (Psalm 105:37).

It is also written:

> *Thy raiment waxed not old upon thee, neither did thy foot swell, these forty years.*
>
> *Deuteronomy 8:4*

The Israelites lived a super healthy life for 40 unbroken years; there was no swelling, no pains and no discomfort. We must recognise that every child of God is a spiritual Jew. It is written: ***But he is a Jew, which is one inwardly; and circumcision is that of the heart, in the spirit, and not in the letter; whose praise is not of men, but of God*** (Romans 2:29).

By redemption, therefore, the great Physician is our Healer ...***for I am the LORD that healeth thee*** (Exodus 15:26). He refers no case to anyone!

Therefore, for sustainable health and vitality, keep living by the Word.

As it is written:

> *My son, attend to my words; incline thine ear unto my sayings. Let them not depart from thine eyes; keep them in the midst of thine heart. For they are life unto those that find them, and health to all their flesh.*
>
> *Proverbs 4:20-22*

We must, thus, place ourselves on a daily dosage of the Word because God's nature is immune to sickness. That is why every Word-addicted person lives a healthy life.

As such, at new birth, our health issues were settled eternally. Remember, ***If the Son therefore shall make you free, ye shall be free indeed*** (John 8:36). I, therefore, decree that every form of satanic oppression on your health ends today, in Jesus' name!

We are Redeemed as Seeds of Abraham!

Christ hath redeemed us from the curse of the law, being made a curse for us: for it is written, Cursed is every one that hangeth on a tree:

That the blessing of Abraham might come on the Gentiles through Jesus Christ; that we might receive the promise of the Spirit through faith.

And if ye be Christ's, then are ye Abraham's seed, and heirs according to the promise.

Galatians 3:13-14, 29 (see also Genesis 22:17-18)

Concerning the Israelites, the Bible says:

When they went from one nation to another, from one kingdom to another people; He suffered no man to do them wrong: yea, he reproved kings for their sakes; Saying, Touch not mine anointed, and do my prophets no harm.

Psalm 105:13-15

Every child of God is, therefore, untouchable because we are spiritual Jews. As seeds of Abraham, by redemption, we are untouchable and 'uncursable'. That means, any pronounced curse on our lives is spiritually illegal. We are 'uncursable' because he that curses us shall be cursed and he that blesses us shall be blessed.

How shall I curse, whom God hath not cursed? or how shall I defy, whom the LORD hath not defied?

Numbers 23:8

For instance, when Abimelech took Sarah, Abraham's wife, everybody in his house became barren! God first closed the womb of everyone in Abimelech's house and, then, appeared to him.

> *...God came to Abimelech in a dream by night, and said to him, Behold, thou art but a dead man, for the woman which thou hast taken; for she is a man's wife.*
>
> *Now therefore restore the man his wife; for he is a prophet, and he shall pray for thee, and thou shalt live: and if thou restore her not, know thou that thou shalt surely die, thou, and all that are thine.*
>
> *Genesis 20:3, 7*

God warned Abimelech to restore Sarah or he and all his household would surely die.

Furthermore, we must understand that we carry generational impact potentials after the order of Abraham. God said to Abraham: *...and in thee shall all the families of the earth be blessed* (Genesis 12:3).

Therefore, every child of God carries the Abrahamic order of potentials that is trans-generational. Remember the Bible says that God is the God of Abraham, Isaac and Jacob! Thus, our lives cannot end here. When our time on earth is over, it must continue after us like Abraham's.

We are to Manifest the Seven Redemptive Treasures in Christ

Saying with a loud voice, Worthy is the Lamb that was slain to receive power, and riches, and wisdom, and strength, and honour, and glory, and blessing.

Revelation 5:12

We must understand that there shall be full manifestations of the seven redemptive treasures in Christ, in these last days. These seven redemptive treasures are clearly summed up in the above scripture and they define our seven-fold redemptive treasures.

Thus, the unleashing of this manifold grace will usher the Church into her golden, triumphant, dominion, mountaintop and heaven-on-earth era. We are, indeed, a people born in due season. Furthermore, we need to know that this is neither by might nor by power but by the agenda of the Spirit of God for the now. We will not miss our place in it!

We are Supernatural Beings

I have said, Ye are gods; and all of you are children of the most High.

Psalm 82:6

Every child of God is a supernatural being and as one, he possesses the nature of God. That means, we carry the ability of God inside us as emphasised in

Psalm 82:6. Jesus also re-emphasised this when he said:

...Is it not written in your law, I said, Ye are gods?
If he called them gods, unto whom the word of God
came, and the scripture cannot be broken.

John 10:34-35

In addition, Jesus is the Lion of the tribe of Judah. Thus, we belong to the lion family. It is, therefore, shameful for the devil, a dog, to be harassing our lives. How can a dog harass a lion? When a lion roars, every animal takes cover.

Friend, in this wicked and wild world, we need a lion's heart to secure our territory. We need to outgrow the sheep nature and become lions or we will be slaughtered. As we all know, the territory of a lion is permanently secured because other beasts keep off and any animal that comes to its territory has presented itself as food for lunch.

However, until we come to terms with this revelation, we may not be able to execute vengeance. Understanding our identity is a prerequisite for executing vengeance on our enemies. Otherwise, when confronted, we will shiver and shift ground several times. That means, if we don't understand our supremacy over the devil, we will remain victims for life and we may suffer what the people in the world suffer. It is the understanding of our supernatural status that puts us in command of situations. Unfortunately, the devil blocks our minds from accessing the light from the Word in order to keep us grounded. It is written: *My people are destroyed for lack of knowledge* (Hosea 4:6). The devil knows that when we have access to light that reveals the truth of our identity, we will take a flight.

The Bible further states:

> *In whom the god of this world hath blinded the minds of them which believe not, lest the light of the glorious gospel of Christ, who is the image of God, should shine unto them.*
>
> *2 Corinthians 4:4*

Ever since I discovered that I am seated in heavenly places in Christ Jesus, I confront challenges with boldness. The truth is that I am not just seated in heavenly places but far above principalities and powers, rulers of this wicked world and wicked spirits in high places. Therefore, when I talk to witches, I talk to them with authority. I have this superiority mentality that the witch that would hurt me is not yet born. The devil knows that if I am coming and he doesn't clear off my way, I will crush him.

We must understand that we are heavenly citizens on an ambassadorial mission on the earth, to reconcile the world to God. An ambassador is an official, who lives in a foreign country as the senior representative of his/her own country. Any assault against him/her is an assault against the nation he represents. Likewise, we are heavenly citizens on ambassadorial mission on earth, resident in the heavenly embassy which is a no-go-area for the things that torture others. That is, though we are in the world, we are not of this world. Therefore, we are untouchable!

We are Commanders of Supernatural Breakthroughs

We are not redeemed to struggle through life. This is because every believer is a spirit being, born as a sign to his world. That is, he is born to live the supernatural life, which is the natural estate of every child of God. As it is written:

> *That which is born of the flesh is flesh; and that which is born of the Spirit is spirit. Marvel not that I said unto thee, Ye must be born again. The wind bloweth where it listeth, and thou hearest the sound thereof, but canst not tell whence it cometh, and whither it goeth: so is every one that is born of the Spirit.*
>
> *John 3:6-8*

However, we must engage our tongues to command the supernatural. The above scripture says, *...and thou hearest the sound thereof...* It takes the sound to command the signs. We understand from the Scripture that Jesus' disciples went forth and preached everywhere, the Lord working with them and confirming the word they spoke (their sounds) with signs following. It is making appropriate sounds (the use of our tongues) that puts us in command of the signs (Mark 16:20).

It is important to know that what we say is what we see; and what we cannot say, we cannot see. Moreover, what we say can completely devalue the revelation we receive from God and His Word. Thus, the signs we command are the products of our words.

Remember, the Bible says:

> **Death and life are in the power of the tongue: and they that love it shall eat the fruit thereof.**
> *Proverbs 18:21 (see also Mark 11:23)*

However, it is not enough to believe it, we must declare it confidently before it can manifest in our lives. The moment we stop saying what we want to see, we will stop seeing it.

As captured in Pastor Yonggi Cho's book, *Ministering Hope For 50 Years*, a renowned Neurosurgeon, in one of his papers, states that the speech area nerve that allows humans to speak has the power to control other parts of the body. For instance, if a person says, **"I am gradually getting weaker,"** other nerves in the body immediately receive that command from the speech area nerve and obey it, saying something like, **"Let's get weak. We need to get weaker; that's the message from the command tower."** That is how a person gets weak and becomes ill. In other words, those nerves can weaken an individual.

However, if an individual says, **"I'm healthy,"** then the speech area nerve sends its command to other nerves, effectively saying, **"You're all healthy."** They respond, **"We're all healthy, very healthy." They then process the command and become healthy**. That way, even sick people can regain their health.

Spiritually, the speech area nerve can be likened to the angels of God, who are sent to minister to us who are heirs of salvation. They are ever on guard to deliver us from evil and carry out our orders, precisely. The Bible says:

> *Suffer not thy mouth to cause thy flesh to sin; neither say thou before the angel, that it was an error: wherefore should God be angry at thy voice, and destroy the work of thine hands?*
>
> *Ecclesiastes 5:6*

Thus, spiritually and scientifically, it is proven that our breakdowns and breakthroughs are absolutely at the command of our tongues.

Therefore, as children of God, we are ordained for unending breakthroughs and the fulfilment of our destinies in grand style (Matthew 11:11, 12:42, 13:54; 1 Corinthians 15:8-10; Psalm 16:6). Nothing will hinder the fulfilment of your destiny, in Jesus' name!

3

---◈---

Price Of Greatness

For which of you, intending to build a tower, sitteth not down first, and counteth the cost, whether he have sufficient to finish it?

Lest haply, after he hath laid the foundation, and is not able to finish it, all that behold it begin to mock him, Saying, This man began to build, and was not able to finish.

Luke 14:28-30

A tower is magnificent in all ramifications; it stands tall and one can't help but notice it. Can you imagine how much it would cost to erect one? Quite a huge amount, coupled with a lot of sacrifices, determination and inconveniences. But a tower is only built when the price is paid and the cost is met. In the same vein, there is a price to pay for every attainment in life and just like an eagle goes through different stages of growth, we have a price to pay for the eagle in us to soar. That means, there is a price attached to every prize.

In the opening scripture, Jesus gave an example of the result of starting something without first counting the cost. Buildings don't just exist, they are built by men, who must first plan carefully and count the cost. Hebrews 3:4 says that "**...every house is builded by some man...**" Towers don't just appear, they are erected. We must know what our towers will cost and be determined to pay the price. Success is not just a dream come true, but a dream made true. Greatness is not just a goodly heritage, it is an attainment. We are children of God and we have a goodly heritage. Psalm 16:6 says: *The lines are fallen unto me in pleasant places; yea, I have a goodly heritage.*

However, to attain this heritage, we must pay the price. Many years ago, I was invited as a guest speaker to a Christian gathering at Warri, in the then Bendel State (Mid-Western region of Nigeria). Due to other pressing engagements, I was unable to go. So, I sent an associate minister with a letter to represent me. When the minister got there with my letter, the people were disappointed but they reluctantly allowed him to minister. At the end of the meeting, this minister was invited to come back for a programme later that year. You see, my letter of recommendation couldn't see him through; he had to earn his way. David earned his way to greatness when he killed Goliath. There is a pathway to greatness; no one succeeds by accident. Deuteronomy 28:1 lays this down: *...if thou shalt hearken diligently unto the voice of the Lord thy God, to observe and to do all his commandments which I command thee this day, that the Lord thy God will set thee on high...*

There is what to hearken to, what to observe and what to do, before we can be "set on high". King Saul did not follow the way of God. He neither hearkened, observed, nor did what God commanded; so, he fell. The pathway to greatness is following God's leading to the letter. Following God in obedience establishes a covenant of greatness, which is the only form of greatness that lasts. When the Lord called me to Ministry, I counted the cost, knew the price I was to pay and went in. To make it impossible for me to make a detour, I burnt the bridge behind me by telling God: *In case I pretend not to have heard You and I want to do other things in life, may I never succeed in those things.*

I had to do this because I knew the price I had to pay might become so magnified in my own eyes that I might turn away from what God had called me to do. I had to burn the bridge behind me because I wanted to obey God, no matter the cost. Jesus is our perfect example; because He wanted to obey His Father, He went through all manner of hardships. He had no house, no family;

he was despised, mocked, flogged and, finally, He had to bear the shame of being hanged naked on the Cross. He died the death of the worst criminal. Why? He wanted "The Tower". Hebrews 12:2 says: *Looking unto Jesus the author and finisher of our faith; who for the joy that was set before him endured the cross, despising the shame, and is set down at the right hand of the throne of God.*

In Philippians 2:6-9, we are told of Jesus:

Who, being in the form of God, thought it not robbery to be equal with God:

But made himself of no reputation, and took upon him the form of a servant, and was made in the likeness of men:

And being found in fashion as a man, he humbled himself, and became obedient unto death, even the death of the cross.

Wherefore God also hath highly exalted him, and given him a name which is above every name.

Jesus was born the Son of God but this was not enough to earn Him automatic greatness. He had to learn obedience to become great. He had to pay the cost for His "Tower". He knew the weight of glory laid before Him and the price He needed to pay to get there. Therefore, He fixed His eyes on the glory and ensured nothing distracted Him. Peter thought He was being of help by telling Him that such hardships were not for Him, but Jesus said: *Get thee behind me, Satan: thou art an offence unto me: for thou savourest not the things that be of God, but those that be of men* (Matthew 16:23).

There is a path to greatness and Jesus took it. He didn't inherit His exalted position, He earned it. He didn't get there by accident; He purchased it by paying the appropriate price. Are you ready to follow suit? Would you take that path to greatness? Then, locate where you want to go and move forward. Consider not the size of the situation; instead, count the cost and be ready to pay the price. Remember, as noted earlier, the eagle doesn't just fly or go about flapping its wings. Rather, it waits for the wind and knows the direction to go; and it rides without stress on the wind. Be strong in the Lord and in the power of His might. Let go of your experiences, abilities and strength; then, look to God in obedience. You will not be a victim of disobedience, in Jesus' name!

It is important to understand that God's plan and purpose for the redeemed is to enjoy unending success. However, God's success plan is not a promise, but a covenant. This implies that until our part is adequately played, God is not committed to deliver. As it is written: *My covenant will I not break, nor alter the thing that is gone out of my lips* (Psalm 89:34; see also Proverbs 4:18; 2 Corinthians 3:18; Luke 5:1-8; John 21:5-6).

Therefore, we must be conscious of our role in the covenant of success. For instance, we understand from the Scripture that when we diligently hearken to biblical instructions and observe to do all that God commands, supernatural breakthrough is usually the outcome. But when the covenant is broken, breakthrough becomes impossible. Therefore, there are certain prices we must pay to make the eaglet in us grow to become an eagle (Deuteronomy 28:1-2; Ecclesiastes 10:5-18).

Let Us Examine Some Vital Prices we Must Pay for the Eagle in us to Emerge

Determination

And they said, Go to, let us build us a city and a tower, whose top may reach unto heaven; and let us make us a name, lest we be scattered abroad upon the face of the whole earth.

And the LORD came down to see the city and the tower, which the children of men builded.

And the LORD said, Behold, the people is one, and they have all one language; and this they begin to do: and now nothing will be restrained from them, which they have imagined to do.

Genesis 11:4-6

If a poll is taken to find out how many people have had their dreams come true, we would discover that they are very few, and these few are those that are at the top, and are still pressing on.

Many people have big dreams but lack the determination to follow through. One of the characteristics of the eagle is determination. It is very tenacious while hunting a prey. It goes after its prey, and grips it firmly when it catches any. It will interest you to know that an eagle can lift a goat in the air and fly with it. Also, when other birds avoid the storm in fear, an eagle spreads its wings and takes advantage of that torrential storm to soar to greater heights.

Likewise, we will experience stormy life situations that may deter us from our God-given assignment. However, like the eagle, we must pay the price of tenacity and face the challenges of life that may stare us in the face. We must also be firm about our goals and remain persistent, refusing to give up, before we can arrive at our destinations.

Champions are not made in dreams; they are made through requisite exercise. For instance, a man who desires to become the world boxing champion must engage in training exercises in his determination to emerge as one. Some athletes spend months in the camp, training, before the actual contest. For a season, they put aside every form of pleasure in order to attain their goals. They refuse and resist all distractions and press on for the prize.

In Philippians 3:14, Paul said: *I press toward the mark for the prize of the high calling of God in Christ Jesus.*

Paul was determined to obtain *the prize for the high calling of God in Christ Jesus*; so, he pressed on. I am sure that many people – including the apostles – would have had a lot of complaints about Paul, but he disregarded every one of them and pressed on. Apart from the spiritual prize he got, some of his physical prizes are evident in the world today; one of which is his documentation of almost half of the New Testament. God used him as much as he allowed himself to be used, through training and fortitude. He put aside everything that could have deterred him from reaching his goal. In Paul's letter to the Church in Philippi, he said:

> *But what things were gain to me, those I counted loss for Christ.*
> *Yea doubtless, and I count all things but loss for the excellency of the knowledge of Christ Jesus my Lord: for whom I have suffered the loss of all things, and do count them but dung, that I may win Christ.*
>
> *Philippians 3:7-8*

Do you have set goals in life? Is there something God has dropped in your mind which you have put aside, saying, "It is impossible?" Friend, if it is from God, then, it cannot be impossible. Remember, when God told the Israelites that the land of Canaan was theirs, the ten spies returned to say that it was impossible because of the giants in the land. There were giants alright, but the people of God still possessed the land because, though their army was inadequate, God empowered them to overcome all the giants. Therefore, we must not drop our God-given ideas because of the economic situation or the state of the stock market. Since the idea is from God, He will provide all that is needed to accomplish it. As such, let's be determined like Joshua and Caleb, and say: ... *Let us go up at once, and possess it; for we are well able to overcome it* (Numbers 13:30).

We are well able, because we are of God. He now dwells in us; we have the Holy Spirit and the mind of Christ and have overcome by reason of the greater One in us. Therefore, let's press on with the ideas God has placed in our hearts and be determined to be the best wherever we are, constantly aiming for the top in our endeavours. Greatness does not just happen; it is earned. So, go and earn yours!

Discipline

Discipline implies possessing a sense of mission in the pursuit of any task. It is strong dedication to a well-defined goal. Apostle Paul said, *Woe is unto me, if I preach not the gospel* (1 Corinthians 9:16).

Also, **it is operating as demanded, not as convenient**. It is submitting to the demands of our set goals. The weight of our tasks determines the kind of efforts we make and the steps we take. For instance, Nehemiah and the people never took off their clothes except for washing. They were on duty as demanded by that task. Daniel and his companions purposed in their hearts not to defile themselves with the king's rich food. We cannot make the most of any task that does not make specific demand on our lives (Nehemiah 4:23; Daniel 1:8).

Furthermore, **discipline is setting order to one's life pursuit**. This means being where we should be at the right time and doing the right thing. For instance, at the time when kings go to battle, David tarried in Jerusalem and he met his waterloo in Bath-sheba. He paid dearly for it, but mercy prevailed for him (2 Samuel 11:1-2).

We must recognise that it takes high-level discipline to maximise our adventure on the earth. No one will ever be more distinguished than he is disciplined. Moreover, we don't know how much we are loaded with, until we set order to our lives.

In addition, **discipline entails making the most of one's time**. We must note that time is the most precious asset to every disciplined man and whatever robs us of our time has robbed us of our best in life. As it is written: *Redeeming the time, because the days are evil* (Ephesians 5:16).

We must budget our time the same way we make budget for our money. Moreover, just like money is squandered when it is not budgeted, when our time is not budgeted, it's bound to be squandered. Benjamin Franklin, one of the founding fathers of America, who was also a believer, once said, "Dost thou love life? Then do not squander time, for that is the stuff life is made of."

It is important to also understand that time is not just in years, but in months, weeks, days, hours, minutes and seconds. Therefore, we must constantly put value into our time by investing it. Interestingly, time is an asset of equality and every living being has an equal share. However, what each one does with his time determines the outcome of his life. That means, we have equal opportunity to make the most of our journey, if we choose to.

On the other hand, self-discipline is being a law to oneself in a bid to accomplish a desired goal. For instance, Nehemiah lived an exemplary life to move the people towards the restoration of their dignity and in 52 days, they completed the building of the wall (Nehemiah 5:14-16; Genesis 39:9; Philippians 2:5-9).

We must recognise that discipline is not a gift, but a lifestyle of choice we design and submit to. This is because no one will ever be more distinguished, in his pursuit, than he is disciplined. Moreover, nothing triggers the potentials within us like self-discipline (Daniel 1:8, 17-20, 6:10-28; 1 Corinthians 6:12, 10:23).

Discipline is obviously a fundamental requirement for exploits and diverse scriptural examples validate this. For instance, **Joseph** was a highly disciplined man and he demonstrated this when he refused to yield to the demands of his master's wife. As a result, he was a highly distinguished man of exploits. He became the breadwinner of nations and the core preserver of Israel. There were no legitimate charges against him, thus, he could be trusted with the entire estate of Potiphar, his master (Genesis 39:9, 21/41:15-16, 38-44).

Daniel purposed in his heart not to defile himself with the king's rich food. As a result, he commanded dominion in Babylon, the land of his captivity. His enemies could not find anything against him, except against the law of his God. He possessed an unusual understanding and wisdom. According to Bible history, Daniel prospered in leadership for 65 years and he remained a revered consultant to every subsequent leader of that nation (Daniel 1:8, 17, 20/5:11/6:1-10, 11-30).

Nehemiah refused to partake of the governor's bread. He led a revolutionary army and was an exemplary leader. He was a man sold-out to his task and the well-being of the people. As a result, he was promoted from a cupbearer to the governor of the nation. We must, therefore, note that our dignity is a function of our discipline (Nehemiah 1:1-10, 4:15-16, 23).

Paul the Apostle was disciplined enough to subscribe to what was profitable. He said: *All things are lawful unto me, but all things are not expedient: all things are lawful for me, but I will not be brought under the power of any* (1 Corinthians 6:12; see also 1 Corinthians 10:23).

He further said: *I keep under my body, and bring it into subjection: lest that by any means, when I have preached to others, I myself should be a castaway* (1 Corinthians 9:27).

It was said of him, "The gods have come down to us in the likeness of men." Even the demons affirmed,

"Jesus, I know; Paul, I know!" He also wrote two-thirds of the New Testament. Therefore, discipline enhances our productivity and it is the highway to distinction in the pursuit of any task (Acts 14:11, 19:14-15; 1 Corinthians 9:24-27).

No doubt, discipline is a fundamental price that must be paid by everyone aspiring to fulfil destiny in grand style. It is the bridle of destiny. It places time check on our persons and helps to maximise our schedules. The best in us comes alive through self-discipline and it is the only way to maintain focus on our assignments.

One of America's founding fathers, George Washington, a devout Christian, said, "Discipline is the soul of an army. It makes small numbers formidable; procures success to the weak, and esteem to all." It is abundantly clear that it takes discipline to pay the extra price for extraordinary accomplishments, to excel in the race of life and be distinguished. The more disciplined we are, the more distinguished we become. Therefore, receive grace for a highly disciplined lifestyle, after the order of Christ, in Jesus' name!

Diligence

"Diligence" here simply means hard work. It is investing the best of one's time, energy and resources in the pursuit of a given task. It is all about hard work, and it is proved that only hard workers ever become high-flyers. It is not just being busy, but being productively engaged and focused in the pursuit of a given task, which is what guarantees outstanding accomplishments (1 Thessalonians 4:11; 1 Peter 4:15; Matthew 6:22).

By much slothfulness the building decayeth; and through idleness of the hands the house droppeth through.

Ecclesiastes 10:18

From the above scripture, we understand that for lack of use, a building runs down and because we are God's building and the temple of the Holy Ghost, our worth can only be enhanced through productive engagement (1 Corinthians 3:9, 6:19). Therefore, just as the physical building depreciates for lack of use, our bodies will begin to decay when we are unproductive. In other words, slothfulness causes decay and makes us smell where we are supposed to shine, due to lack of adequate productive engagement. This implies that we continuously lose value when we are not adequately engaged. On the other hand, our values will continue to be enhanced through diligence. Remember, it is written, *In all labour there is profit: but the talk of the lips tendeth only to penury* (Proverb 14:23).

However, no one hates to become a star; it is the price that scares many. But, as we all know, no one can get out of life more than what he puts into it, because whatsoever a man sows that shall he reap. This is why diligence is a universal demand for anyone who desires success in life and nothing else can be a substitute for that (Galatians 6:7; 2 Corinthians 9:6).

Furthermore, diligence is one of the keys to the restoration of our human dignity, because the sluggard is sure to end up a failure (Proverbs 12:24, 13:4, 20:4, 24:30-34).

There is no success story, either in the Scripture or in modern times, without a demonstration of diligence.

Let's Examine Some Scriptural Examples of Men Who Worked Their Way to the Top

- **Abraham:** He was a hard worker. When God told him, "I will make you great," he worked his way up by engaging in cattle farming until he became the greatest cattle farmer of his time.

   And Abram was very rich in cattle, in silver, and in gold. ...And Abraham was old, and well stricken in age: and the Lord had blessed Abraham in all things (Genesis 13:2, 24:1).

   Subsequently, the Bible admonishes us to do the works of Abraham in order to partake of the Abrahamic order of blessings. Therefore, we must engage in productive labour throughout the days of our lives, if we must flow in the blessings of Abraham (John 8:39; Isaiah 51:1-3).

- **Isaac:** He was a **tireless worker**. He dug wells for irrigation, but the Philistines kept filling them up. Notwithstanding, he continued digging until he wearied them. Thus, he invented irrigation farming and became the breadwinner of the nation. He became a great employer of labour, while others were waiting for rain.

As it is written: ***Then, Isaac sowed in that land, and received in the same year an hundredfold: and the Lord blessed him. And the man waxed great, and went forward, and grew until he became very great: For he had possession of flocks, and possessions of herds, and great store of servants: and the Philistines envied him*** (Genesis 26:12-14; see also Genesis 26:1-13).

Remember, the Bible says: ***...we, brethren, as Isaac was, are the children of promise*** (Galatians 4:28). It implies that by redemption, we are ordained to be envied, like Isaac, but only on the platform of hard work. Therefore, as we engage diligently in our endeavours, we shall not be stranded or pitied anymore!

- **Jacob:** He was a **creative worker**. When Laban played on Jacob's intelligence, his ingenuity and creativity brought him out, because he knew what to do to beat

Laban hands down (Genesis 30:27-37). Thus, Jacob prevailed through creative labour.

As it is written, *And the man increased exceedingly, and had much cattle, and maidservants, and menservants, and camels, and asses* (Genesis 30:43). Therefore, receive grace for creative labour, in the name of Jesus!

• **Paul:** Although a man of unusual revelation, endowed with the Spirit of faith and grace, yet, Paul said, *...but I laboured more abundantly than they all: yet not I, but the grace of God which was with me* (1 Corinthians 15:10).

He laboured and emerged a star among the Apostles. As a result, he wrote two-thirds of the New Testament; he was indeed God's wisdom in human flesh (1 Corinthians 9:16; Acts 14:11, 19:14-15; 2 Peter 3:15).

Therefore, it is labour that gives value to grace. This is because one can frustrate or receive the grace of God in vain through slothfulness (1 Corinthians 15:10).

• **Joseph:** After Joseph was sold into slavery in Egypt, he could have despaired of life and let go but he didn't. Everywhere Joseph found himself, he was diligent in his business with all godliness.

How did Joseph, a stranger and a servant, rise to the top in his master's house? The Bible says that *Joseph went to do his business* (Genesis 39:11). He refused to be distracted. He was focused on his assignment. There must have been other servants, but neither they nor Potiphar's wife could deter him. Even in prison, Joseph still rose to the top. The Bible says:

> **And the keeper of the prison committed to Joseph's hand all the prisoners that were in the prison; and whatsoever they did there, he was the doer of it.**
>
> *Genesis 39:22*

He knew God was with him. This, coupled with his diligence and determination to please God, made him rise to the top echelon of government in Egypt. He was a stranger who became a Prime Minister in a foreign country. Joseph paved his way to greatness; it didn't just happen. If Joseph, a slave, could make it in a foreign country because God was with him, then, all our excuses should be dropped in the trash can.

Furthermore, God, our heavenly Father, is an ever-working God. Recently checking through God's work schedule at creation, I discovered that it was an affair of the evening and the morning. As it is written, ***And the evening and the morning were the first day*** (Genesis 1:5), as it is written, ***And the evening and the morning were the second day*** (Genesis 1:8), as it is written, ***And the evening and the morning were the third day*** (Genesis 1:13), etc. It appears that God works 24 hours;

no wonder the Bible says, "He that keepeth Israel shall neither slumber nor sleep" (Psalm 121:4).

Again, we saw Jesus our Saviour, a tireless worker, who was ever on duty because working was like eating to Him. For instance, Jesus said, *My meat is to do the will of him that sent me, and to finish his work* (John 4:34).

Again, He said, *I must work the works of him that sent me, while it is day: the night cometh, when no man can work* (John 9:4).

From these scriptures, we understand that work was a must for Christ, not an option. He was addicted to His mission and gave His all to fulfil it.

Furthermore, the Bible admonishes us to walk in the steps of Christ, which implies working as Christ worked. Remember, nobody ever emerges a giant without walking in the steps of giants; and it is the quality of our work that defines our overall worth (1 Peter 2:21).

In addition, we must understand that there is no substitute for work. For instance, the anointing is not a substitute, because Jesus was anointed without measure, yet He was a hard worker. Revelation is not a substitute, because Jesus is the Living Word personified and the ultimate of revelations. Faith is not a substitute, because faith without works is dead. Remember, Jesus is the Author and Finisher of our faith (John 3:34, 1:1-5; Hebrews 12:1-2).

Furthermore, Jesus said, "It is finished," because He completed the mission for which He came. Paul also said, "I have finished my course." Therefore, it is possible to finish God's mission for us on earth (John 19:30; 2 Timothy 4:7).

What, then, are the Benefits of Diligence?

Diligence keeps us physically fit

It is important to understand that hard work does not kill; it only refines our lives and destinies. For instance, when a house is left unoccupied for a period of time, it begins to drop in value and rodents invade and occupy it. Similarly, when we stop working, several things begin to creep into our lives. This is why when people stop working, they start to lose value. Therefore, staying on our jobs keeps us fit, apart from the success and exploits that come our way through hard work (Ecclesiastes 10:18).

It engenders excellence

For every one that useth milk is unskilful in the word of righteousness: for he is a babe. But strong meat belongeth to them that are of full age, even those who by reason of use have their senses exercised to discern both good and evil.

Hebrews 5:13-14

There is nothing mystical about excellence; it is a product of **man's tireless commitment to improvement**. This is why excellence is an end-product of diligence (Proverbs 22:29).

Diligence delivers us from some awful vices of life

Let him that stole steal no more: but rather let him labour, working with his hands the thing which is good, that he may have to give to him that needeth.

Ephesians 4:28

If you are not a worker, you will end up a thief. Remember, Jesus said, "...Occupy till I come." Therefore, if we must be fulfilled, then we must be productively engaged in our various endeavours (Luke 19:13; Proverb 14:23).

It is important to know that many destinies are tied to ours; thus, we cannot afford to be slothful and irresponsible. If we fail, we would disappoint God, because He has paid every price required for us to have good success. Therefore, we must wake up and take responsibility for a highly productive life that will turn us into men and women of exploits.

Sacrifice

Jesus said:

Verily, verily, I say unto you, Except a corn of wheat fall into the ground and die, it abideth alone: but if it die, it bringeth forth much fruit. He that loveth his life shall lose it; and he that hateth his life in this world shall keep it unto life eternal. If any man serve me, let him follow me; and where I am, there shall also my servant be: if any man serve me, him will my Father honour.

John 12:24-26

Sacrifice is a universal demand for the making of stars and it is impossible to emerge a star in life without embracing the law of sacrifice. No wonder Martin Luther King Jnr said, "Every step towards the goal of justice requires sacrifice."

I have often said, "There there is no star without a scar and the scar of every star is sacrifice" (Luke 12:49-50; Philippians 1:21).

Sacrifice, in this context, **is denying ourselves of certain comfort and pleasure, for the success of an assignment or a goal**.

Then said Jesus unto his disciples, If any man will come after me, let him deny himself, and take up his cross, and follow me.

Matthew 16:24

Furthermore, **it is going beyond one's best to achieve a given task**. Doing our best in the pursuit of a particular goal is diligence; but going beyond our best is sacrifice. This is because there is nothing extraordinary on its own; it is man's extraordinary input that makes it so (2 Corinthians 6:3-10).

However, there are certain **fundamentals of sacrifice** that we must be acquainted with.

* **Sacrifice is a choice:** Sacrifice is not a gift, but a choice. It is the choice of the wise. As it is written:

  I call heaven and earth to record this day against you, that I have set before you life and death, blessing and cursing: therefore choose life, that both thou and thy seed may live.

  Deuteronomy 30:19

Remember, we are presented with choices daily, which either move us up on the success ladder or otherwise. However, the right decisions that move us up the success ladder always require sacrifice.

* **Sacrifice commands rewards and benefits:** The benefits of sacrifice always outweigh its cost. Many want the success, but they don't like the sacrifice because they forget that the cost is never greater than the glory. That's why whenever it's time to sacrifice, we must ignore the present and look to the future.

For instance, Jesus for the joy that was set before Him endured the inconveniences of the cross, the beatings and the pains so that we can be partakers of His glory (Hebrews 12:1-2).

- **Sacrifice requires putting our body under subjection:** Apostle Paul said: *But I keep under my body, and bring it into subjection: lest that by any means, when I have preached to others, I myself should be a castaway* (1 Corinthians 9:27; see also 1 Corinthians 15:31).

He further said:

> *I am crucified with Christ: nevertheless I live; yet not I, but Christ liveth in me: and the life which I now live in the flesh I live by the faith of the Son of God, who loved me, and gave himself for me.*
>
> *Galatians 2:20*

It takes the cup of wisdom and the baptism of sacrifice to emerge a success in any of life's endeavours.

Meekness

> *Blessed are the meek: for they shall inherit the earth.*
>
> *Matthew 5:5*

Meekness is a priceless treasure because it defines greatness. Concerning Moses, one of the greatest men who ever lived, the Bible says that he was the meekest of all men in his days. As it is written:

Now the man Moses was very meek, above all the men which were upon the face of the earth.

Numbers 12:3

For instance, despite the fact that Moses saw God face-to-face, divided the Red Sea and performed strange works by God's hand, Jethro (his father-in-law) could still counsel him. Jethro, the Priest of Midian, was Moses' coach, and Moses hearkened unto him. It is the quality of our meekness that defines the limits of our greatness.

The Spirit of meekness at work in Moses gave him his unique place in destiny. Moses was so great that when he spoke of Jesus in prophecy, he said:

The LORD thy God will raise up unto thee a Prophet from the midst of thee, of thy brethren, like unto me; unto him ye shall hearken.

Deuteronomy 18:15 (see also Acts 3:20-22)

Jesus came like unto Moses and He said, *...I am meek and lowly in heart...* (Matthew 11:29). In Luke chapter 9, Moses and Elijah appeared to Jesus on the Mountain of Transfiguration and spoke with Him. That was how great Moses was, but meekness was the foundation of his greatness.

The treasure of meekness is one of the vital treasures in the making of any Kingdom star. In fact, the Bible defines the virtue of meekness as an ornament of great price.

> **But let it be the hidden man of the heart, in that which is not corruptible, even the ornament of a meek and quiet spirit, which is in the sight of God of great price.**
>
> *1 Peter 3:4*

The enlargement of any star in the Kingdom is limited by his degree of meekness. Therefore, meekness is a blessing; pride, on the other hand, is a curse. Remember that God resists the proud but He gives more grace to the humble (James 4:6). That means, meekness grants us access to more grace. It is grace that makes great. Paul said: **But by the grace of God I am what I am** (1 Corinthians 15:10). Many people have lost their destinies to pride, which has shut them out of grace. For instance, satan lost his leadership place to pride. No doubt, the treasure of meekness is the covenant gateway to greatness. It opens us to grace, which makes great and unveils to us insight that makes high fliers. You will not lose your place in destiny to pride, in Jesus' name!

Let's recognise that Christianity is all about accepting

spiritual responsibilities. Responsibility is all about responding positively to the demands placed on us by our task or pursuit. However, when we refuse or ignore responsibility, we become liabilities. It is not enough to know that we have a heritage of greatness in redemption; we must accept responsibility for its actualisation.

Winston Churchill said, "The price of greatness is responsibility." Our behaviour will definitely reflect what we see ahead of us. A playboy today will, at best, end up a play-man tomorrow. However, a serious-minded young man or lady today is another star in the making. We are that star the Lord is talking about! Let us, therefore, take responsibility!

4

Making A Difference

And they shall be mine, saith the LORD of hosts, in that day when I make up my jewels; and I will spare them, as a man spareth his own son that serveth him. Then shall ye return, and discern between the righteous and the wicked, between him that serveth God and him that serveth him not.

Malachi 3:17-18

God created the earth and all that is in it. There are princes and there are servants. If you are born again, you are a child of the King; therefore, you are either a Prince or Princess.

I have seen servants upon horses, and princes walking as servants upon the earth.

Ecclesiastes 10:7

The unbelievers are the servants because they are strangers to the Kingdom of God and the Scripture says:

Thou hast delivered me from the strivings of the

people; and thou hast made me the head of the heathen: a people whom I have not known shall serve me.

As soon as they hear of me, they shall obey me: the strangers shall submit themselves unto me.

The strangers shall fade away, and be afraid out of their close places.

Psalm 18:43-45

God made us the head while unbelievers are to be our servants. If servants ride on horses while we walk, we made the choice to do so. We must have chosen to let them have the horses because it is the instructions given to one's servants that he/she obeys. Can you imagine a servant going to take the master's car and driving it about while the master goes about on foot? No! This can only be possible if the servant is not put in his proper position in which case, it is not the servant's fault but that of the master. Therefore, if we are not riding our 'horses', it is our fault.

The reason some Christians look more beloved than others is in the individual persons. While one is an escapist, the other is a contestant. The escapist sees a hurdle and carefully avoids it. Perhaps, he tried and failed yesterday and is haunted by the memories of his past failures. The contestant, on the other hand, welcomes combats. He goes in the strength of the

Lord and overcomes. He is fearless because he knows that *...a just man falleth seven times, and riseth up again...* (Proverbs 24:16).

The lines are fallen for us in pleasant places because we are sons and heirs of God. We have a common and great inheritance in God. Our God is rich in glory. He is a rich God because the whole earth and its fullness are His. He owns all the cattle on a thousand hills and all the silver and gold are His. Being heirs, therefore, we have the unreserved right of tapping into God's abundance. Furthermore, we all have glorious destinies in God.

It is written:

> *For whom he did foreknow, he also did predestinate to be conformed to the image of his Son, that he might be the firstborn among many brethren.*
> *Moreover whom he did predestinate, them he also called: and whom he called, them he also justified: and whom he justified, them he also glorified.*
> *Romans 8:29-30*

Everyone in the faith is there for glorification. Also, everyone in the Kingdom is called because no one comes to the Son, Jesus, without the **Father** drawing him. Therefore, if God called us, then **He has** justified us to enter the realm of glorification. To those who obey God's commandments, He says they shall be set on high. We shall be the head and not the tail.

There is an adage which says: "No venture; no success." The escapist does not venture; instead, he dodges responsibilities and becomes a loser. He does not like changes; therefore, he accepts everything that comes as the will of God. He is settled in his position; as a result, he neither has vision nor goals. The Bible says: *Where there is no vision, the people perish...* (Proverbs 29:18).

Without a target, there is no driving force. Where there is no motivation, there will be no pressing. Pressing comes with a vision, which leads to attainment. It is written:

> *And from the days of John the Baptist until now the kingdom of heaven suffereth violence, and THE VIOLENT TAKE IT BY FORCE.*
>
> Matthew 11:12 (Emphasis mine)

> *The law and the prophets were until John: since that time the kingdom of God is preached, and EVERY MAN PRESSETH INTO IT.*
>
> Luke 16:16 (Emphasis mine)

For us to acquire these treasures, we must press (put pressure upon); but if we don't have a vision of these treasures, we will lack the propelling force. As a result, one becomes a wishful thinker – a dreamer, while the other, a dream activator. The wishful thinker makes up grandiose dreams but does not activate them. Proverbs 13:4 says: *The soul of the sluggard desireth, and hath nothing: but the soul of the diligent shall be made fat.*

He is a sluggard, who likes to sleep and dream; therefore, he has nothing to show. Poverty becomes his surname. If you are a dreamer, the Bible is talking to you expressly in the following scriptures:

> *How long wilt thou sleep, O sluggard? when wilt thou arise out of thy sleep?*
>
> *Yet a little sleep, a little slumber, a little folding of the hands to sleep:*
>
> *So shall thy poverty come...*
>
> Proverbs 6:9-11

The dream activator is only made fat because *he that tilleth his land shall be satisfied with bread* (Proverbs 12:11). He that activates his dreams shall be satisfied with plenty. The sluggard, because of his laziness, always has reasons for his sluggishness and inaction. In the parable of the talents, the servant who received one talent had his reasons for not investing it and to him, they were very good reasons. He is *wiser in his own conceit than seven men that can render a reason* (Proverbs 26:16).

The sluggard has seemingly beautiful reasons like: "The situation in the country today is just terrible." "Jesus is coming very soon, so there is no need for new projects; I'll make do with the ones I have." He keeps on "making do" until Jesus comes. He is the one who will say, **There is a lion in the way; a lion is in the streets** (Proverbs 26:13). He is also the one who will not plough by reason of the cold. Unfortunately, the Scripture says, he shall *beg in harvest and have nothing* (Proverbs 20:4).

If Isaac had considered the difficult farming conditions in the land of the Philistines, he would not have sowed. Rather, he disregarded the weather conditions and regarded only his God to sow, and God blessed him as he reaped a hundredfold. Isaac was a dream activator and a contestant.

There is no future for a slothful man. The Bible says that his way *is an hedge of thorns* and he shall continually *be under tribute* (Proverbs 12:24). In other words, he is destined for failure. Instead of ruling, he shall continually be a servant and the diligent man shall rule over him. Where he is meant to soar like the eagle, he shall fall to the ground and be trodden under the feet of men.

God has prepared a glorious end for everyone who is in Christ Jesus. That means, if you are in school, the end of your schooling will be glorious. If you are in business, the operations of your business will be transformed from one degree of glory to another. In fact, every child of God has the same glorious heritage, because the Scripture says:

There is one body, and one Spirit, even as ye are called in one hope of your calling; One Lord, one faith, one baptism, One God and Father of all, who is above all, and through all, and in you all.

Ephesians 4:4-6

We are of one body with Christ, the Glorious Head; therefore, the body is glorious. Think of this: if we are all children and heirs of God, then, why the difference in status? If we are of one body, one shepherd, one faith and one baptism, why the difference among the sheep? If we have all been accepted in the beloved, why do some look more "beloved" than others? I know you are saying right now in your heart: "All fingers are not equal!" Yes, all fingers may not be equal, but all those who are called are equal before God, Who called them. The difference, therefore, is not in God because He is no respecter of persons. The Scripture tells us in Acts 10:34-35:

...Of a truth I perceive that God is no respecter of persons:

But in every nation he that feareth him, and worketh righteousness, is accepted with him.

It did not say the white nations alone but, "In every nation" – green, white, red, black, yellow – "every nation". It doesn't matter what nation you are from;

your colour is insignificant. As long as you fear and love God, He is able, willing and happy to take you to heights yet unknown. For instance, the Scripture says that God delights in the prosperity of His servants.

> *...Let the LORD be magnified, which hath pleasure in the prosperity of his servant.*
>
> *Psalm 35:27*

Think of this: which father will want his child to go hungry when he has all it takes for the child to live a hunger-free life? Also, which father would like to see his child looking wretched and languishing in poverty? None! Therefore, if earthly parents provide for their children and always want them to stand out at every function; how much more God, Who has all things in His hands?

He delights in our prosperity, which means, He is unhappy at our poverty. He wants all His children to be happy and prosperous; He wants them to stand out as ensigns in the world. He wants to take them to great heights beyond their imagination. In 1 Corinthians 2:9, the Bible says:

> *Eye hath not seen, nor ear heard, neither have entered into the heart of man, the things which God hath prepared for them that love him.*

Do you love God? Are you accepted by Him? If your

answer is "Yes", then, you are destined for a great future, because God's Word cannot be broken. He abides faithful and cannot deny Himself. He has said:

My covenant will I not break, nor alter the thing that is gone out of my lips.

Psalm 89:34

If God truly said all that is written about us in the Bible and the scripture cannot be broken, then why are some still downtrodden? Why are some believers still at the bottom of the ladder, while others are up and pressing on?

Remember, we are in a race and there are no middle places. We are either winners or losers. We are in a warfare; therefore, we must be prepared to win just as a conqueror must be prepared to conquer. If you want to soar above the storms of life, then, take the path of the eagle — be determined not to fall when thrown, but to soar. Count the cost and bear your cross to win the crown. Remember, we are children of the King; thus, we are born to reign. We are ordained to be at the top, not at the bottom. The heathens are meant to see the glory of the Lord upon us; therefore, RISE UP AND SHOW FORTH THE GLORY OF THE LORD!

5

The Eagle's Anointing

How God anointed Jesus of Nazareth with the Holy Ghost and with power: who went about doing good, and healing all that were oppressed of the devil; for God was with him.

Acts 10:38

God is the Source of empowerment and grace, and only those who know how to get into His presence ever get imparted and 'engraced'. People who flow under fresh oil are those who know how to engage God's presence. The Bible says:

Come unto me, all ye that labour and are heavy laden, and I will give you rest. Take my yoke upon you, and learn of me; for I am meek and lowly in heart: and ye shall find rest unto your souls. For my yoke is easy, and my burden is light.

Matthew 11:28-30

God's commandments are not grievous. The way to

scaling new heights is not tough; it just requires us to make a discovery of it. Most of the time, people are waiting to be touched and for hands to be laid on them before they are imparted with grace. That is why people miss the opportunities for impartation. Impartations are principally conveyed through words. The most profound impartations of my life didn't come by laying on of hands, but by the Word. It is written:

> *And the spirit entered into me when he spake unto me, and set me upon my feet, that I heard him that spake unto me.*
>
> *Ezekiel 2:2*

I was imparted with grace to love God, by His Word. Nobody laid hands on me but the Spirit of love overwhelmed me by an encounter from the book, *The Man God Uses* by Oswald J. Smith. I got married to Jesus from that encounter and that marriage has been the sweetest experience of my life. Oswald J. Smith was about to die at that time; so, I never saw him.

Also, it was an encounter with the Word of the Lord in T. L. Osborn's book that caused my spiritual ears to pop open.

The Bible says:

> *...he wakeneth morning by morning, he wakeneth mine ear to hear as the learned. The Lord God hath*

opened mine ear, and I was not rebellious, neither turned away back.

Isaiah 50:4-5

Jesus, the Master Eagle said: *I can of mine own self do nothing: as I hear...* (John 5:30). Therefore, if we are unable to hear, we are not candidates for the flight.

In 1982, I encountered the Word of grace that destroyed every trace of poverty mentality and brought me into realms of unspeakable financial fortune, even without having a dime.

In 1986, Kenneth E. Hagin was speaking at a convention and I was sitting at the gallery when the power of God hit me. That encounter turned our ministry around.

The Covenant Platform for the Rise of Eagles

For the Lord's portion is his people; Jacob is the lot of his inheritance. He found him in a desert land, and in the waste howling wilderness; he led him about, he instructed him, he kept him as the apple of his eye. As an eagle stirreth up her nest, fluttereth over her young, spreadeth abroad her wings, taketh them, beareth them on her wings: So the Lord alone did lead him, and there was no strange god with him. He made him ride on the high places of the earth, that he might eat the increase of the fields;

and he made him to suck honey out of the rock, and oil out of the flinty rock.

Deuteronomy 32:9-13

The above scripture depicts affluence, relevance, dignity, honour and impact. The Eagle's anointing begins with a revelation of our portion and inheritance in Christ. Our journey to scaling new heights begins with a clear revelation of our inheritances. If that is our portion, how much of it have we discovered? Remember in Matthew 11:11, Jesus said:

> *Verily I say unto you, Among them that are born of women there hath not risen a greater than John the Baptist: notwithstanding he that is least in the kingdom of heaven is greater than he.*

In other words, every child of God carries potentials that far outweigh the greatest potentials in the Old Testament. Therefore, within us lie redemptive deposits that make us greater than the greatest names in the Old Testament.

We are ordained for unlimited heights. Therefore, when we see our future through God's eyes, we cannot be depressed. In 1984, I saw our ministry on top of the world, though there was nothing to show for it at that time. Jesus came and blew it up from John 14:12:

> *Verily, verily, I say unto you, He that believeth on me, the works that I do shall he do also; and greater works*

than these shall he do; because I go unto my Father.

That means, we are to exceed where Jesus stopped and He has not stopped manifesting till today. He is still impacting the world in greater dimensions than when He walked the earth, and He said that we will do greater than He did.

We must recognise that we are redeemed to make impact, not just a living. Furthermore, it is not a "now" impact, but a generational and trans-generational one. That means, one generation after another will be talking about our impact! Therefore, the eagle's anointing begins with the Spirit of revelation which unveils who we are, what we are worth and what we can do in Christ.

However, it takes the leading of the Spirit of God to be empowered to scale new heights. Deuteronomy 32:12 says that **the Lord alone did lead him**. Also, the army of high flyers described in Joel 2:1-11 was an unusual army because it was led by the Spirit of God. The world has never seen its kind and the Bible says that neither will there be any after such until the years of many generations. As it is written:

> **...a great people and a strong; there hath not been ever the like, neither shall be any more after it, even to the years of many generations... They shall run like mighty men; they shall climb the wall like men of war; and they shall march every one on his ways,**

and they shall not break their ranks ... they shall walk everyone in his path ... And the Lord shall utter his voice before his army: for his camp is very great: for he is strong that executeth his word ...

Joel 2:2-11

This is a description of an army of visionaries who are record 'breakers' and 'setters'.

Many years ago, one of my friends who had a very powerful ministry in a part of Nigeria said to me: "Brother David, I'm going to Lagos." I asked, "What about?" He replied, "All the money in Nigeria is in Lagos." Eventually, he lost everything to being led by strange gods. It is a sad story. He went to where all the money in Nigeria was, but only incurred the kind of debt that he had never imagined before.

Don't jump at a job because the offer is attractive; instead, go there because you know that is where you belong. Today, many people have gone out of their countries to various places where they don't belong. Remember, as many as are led by the Spirit of God, they are the sons of God. Consider the beauty of Moses' ministry. It was all about: "And the Lord said unto Moses." He was perpetually led into strange dimensions of greatness. And Moses was a great man in the land of Egypt before Pharaoh and all his servants. In fact, God said to him:

See, I have made thee a god to Pharaoh: and Aaron

thy brother shall be thy prophet.

Exodus 7:1

God said to Miriam, "Are you not afraid to speak against My servant? If there be a prophet among you, Moses is not in his class! I speak with him face-to-face." Moses was led to strange dimensions of heights by God. In fact, God had to bury him by Himself. Also, God told Abraham, "Get thee out of thy country..." He was led into trans-generational greatness and he scaled unusual heights. God led him in chapters 12, 17 and 22. It is impossible to be led by God and still be grounded, because all the forces of heaven always back the led. When God leads, He goes before us to destroy the barriers on our paths. He also goes with us to ensure that nothing is against us.

Also, when God leads, He works with us.

As it is written:

And they went forth, and preached every where, the Lord working with them, and confirming the word with signs following.

Mark 16:20

When God leads, He works through us. The Bible says: For it is God which worketh in you both to will and to do of his good pleasure.

Philippians 2:13

Furthermore, when God leads us, He works for us. The scripture says: **Faithful is he that calleth you, who also will do it** (1 Thessalonians 5:24). That is why we cannot be thoroughly led, and not scale new heights. Therefore, I decree spiritual deafness to be healed today!

The Bible further says:

> **For as many as are led by the Spirit of God, they are the sons of God.**
>
> Romans 8:14

Concerning Jacob, the Bible records:

> **He found him in a desert land, and in the waste howling wilderness; he led him about, he instructed him, he kept him as the apple of his eye.**
>
> Deuteronomy 32:10

We must never allow where we are to blindfold us from what awaits us. Where we are is immaterial; where we are going is more important.

It is written:

> **Though thy beginning was small, yet thy latter end should greatly increase.**
>
> Job 8:7

> **For who hath despised the day of small things?...**
>
> Zechariah 4:10

We must understand that every great thing starts

small. For instance, no child weighs 20 kilograms at birth. Every baby is born weighing few kilograms and then, increases in weight. Similarly, someone who is called a Nobel Laureate today was an ordinary pupil some years ago. It was by dint of hard work coupled with a vision of where he desired to be; and one step after the other, he got there. Thus, let's not allow our present state to rob us of our great future. The Bible says:

> *Behold my servant, whom I uphold; mine elect, in whom my soul delighteth; I have put my spirit upon him: he shall bring forth judgment to the Gentiles. He shall not fail nor be discouraged, till he have set judgment in the earth: and the isles shall wait for his law.*
>
> *Isaiah 42:1, 4*

Therefore, receive the anointing for courage! You shall not fail or be discouraged in the adventure of life! It is courage that makes conquerors and champions are made out of challenges.

> *I have taught thee in the way of wisdom; I have led thee in right paths.*
>
> *Take fast hold of instruction; let her not go: keep her; for she is thy life.*
>
> *Proverbs 4:11, 13*

The worth of our lives is a function of the quality of instructions we operate in. It is written:

And it shall come to pass, if thou shalt hearken diligently unto the voice of the Lord thy God, to observe and to do all his commandments which I command thee this day, that the Lord thy God will set thee on high above all nations of the earth.

Deuteronomy 28:1

When we operate by the instructions of the Most High God, we will continue to scale new heights as a lifestyle. Jesus said, *I can of mine own self do nothing: as I hear, I judge...* (John 5:30). We need those instructions to soar like the eagle. For instance, there is nowhere Lagos is mentioned in the Bible, but God said to me, "Arise, get down to Lagos, and raise me a people." There is nothing called Africa in the Bible, but God told me, "Now, the harvest of Africa is overripe, rush in and preserve it from decadence." These are all specific instructions that created platforms for next levels.

Furthermore, we must subject ourselves to required exercises for the eagle in us to come alive. The Bible says:

And the child grew, and waxed strong in spirit, and was in the deserts till the day of his shewing unto Israel.

Luke 1:80

Paul also said:

> *But refuse profane and old wives' fables, and exercise thyself rather unto godliness. For bodily exercise profiteth little: but godliness is profitable unto all things, having promise of the life that now is, and of that which is to come.*
>
> *1 Timothy 4:7-8*

This further validates the truth that we need spiritual exercises to excel in life and that takes discipline. I was addicted to spiritual exercises and I undertook fasting adventures, coupled with prayers, not for "bread and butter" but to be 'engraced' to fulfil destiny. Meanwhile, I had no idea that I would be called to ministry. We must understand that no one ever excels in anything in which he does not exercise himself. When we excel spiritually, we excel in life. That is why the Bible says that to be carnally minded is death but to be spiritually minded is life and peace (Romans 8:6).

Concerning Jesus, the Bible says:

> *The child grew, and waxed strong in spirit, and was in the deserts till the day of his shewing unto Israel.*
>
> *Luke 1:80*

Jesus was exercising Himself spiritually, until the day of His showing forth to Israel.

I went on a fasting expedition to read the book of the

Acts of Apostles. Is it that the grammar is too tough? No! Life is a product of personal adventure. We are 75% responsible for everything that takes place in our lives. This is because every time we point a finger at someone, we point three at ourselves. Everybody, including God is just 25%; we are 75% responsible for the outcome of our lives. Therefore, we either take responsibilities or we die as liabilities!

Just imagine the part a coach plays in the life of a sportsman and you will understand this. The coach tells the sportsman what to do, but he doesn't do it for him; instead, he leaves him to do it. Receive grace today to exercise yourself adequately for the eagle in you to emerge!

Our Father God is an Eagle

An Eagle cannot beget a vulture because only like begets like. As many as received Christ, He gave power to become the sons of God. Therefore, if God, our Father, is an Eagle and we are born again children of God, we cannot be ducks. According to Scripture, everything produces after its kind: human beings don't give birth to ducks, and ducks can't give birth to human beings.

If the Father God is the Eagle God, then all His children must be eagles. Hence, we have an Eagle root in God and that establishes the fact that we are ordained to keep scaling new heights. Eagles are never found roaming the streets; they are always in the sky. Therefore, from now, we will not be found in the low places of life again!

We Also Have an Eagle Saviour

Speaking of Jesus in prophecy, the Bible says:

> *For Moses truly said unto the fathers, A prophet shall the Lord your God raise up unto you of your brethren, like unto me; him shall ye hear in all things whatsoever he shall say unto you.*
>
> *Acts 3:22*

God said:

> *Ye have seen what I did unto the Egyptians, and how I bare you on eagles' wings, and brought you unto myself. Now therefore, if ye will obey my voice indeed, and keep my covenant, then ye shall be a peculiar treasure unto me above all people: for all the earth is mine.*
>
> *Exodus 19:4-5*

That means, Jesus came as our Eagle Saviour and Hebrews 2:11 records that *He is not ashamed to call us brethren*. Therefore, the Father God is the Eagle Father. His begotten Son, Jesus, is the Eagle Son and He is not afraid to call us brethren; thus, we are His siblings. Consequently, we are eagles after the order of Christ because there is no way a vulture can be the brother of an eagle.

There is an eagle in us and we are ordained to soar in the sky, not to struggle on earth. From today, receive the soaring impartation on your life!

Our greatest asset as eagles is revelation. As we go from revelation to revelation, we also go from glory to glory.

The Word says:

> **But we all, with open face beholding as in a glass the glory of the Lord, are changed into the same image from glory to glory, even as by the Spirit of the Lord.**
>
> *2 Corinthians 3:18*

Also, it is written:

> **...but the people that do know their God shall be strong, and do exploits.**
>
> *Daniel 11:32*

That means, the more revelation of God the Father we have, the more exploits we are qualified to command. Somebody read one of my books, *Towards Mental Exploits*, and jumped from failure to a first class student. It is our findings that define our future. The farther we see, the more heights we scale.

Before my wife and I got married, I read eight books on marriage and made outstanding discoveries that levelled out any apprehension on what the outcome of our marriage would be. Coming into ministry, I read 39 biographies of great ministries so I could understand how ministry operates. Also, before Covenant University started, I studied nine World Class Universities, their founding history, developmental processes, programmes, etc. Thereafter, I drafted the philosophy and core values of Covenant University; and with this, I was ready to fly. Today, Covenant University is flying. It has consistently been number one among private universities, since the National Universities Commission (NUC) appraisal began.

God cannot confirm the word we are yet to find. It is our discoveries that lead the way to recoveries. Scaling new heights only comes by taking responsibility, not by chanting it as a slogan. We do not scale new heights by waiting, but by working. Furthermore, we cannot scale new heights without adequately engaging spirituality, to generate sufficient ground power that empowers us to overcome gravity and take off into the skies.

The Role of Spirituality

This book of the law shall not depart out of thy mouth; but thou shalt meditate therein day and night, that thou mayest observe to do according to all that is written therein: for then thou shalt make thy way prosperous, and then thou shalt have good success.

Joshua 1:8

Spirituality is our greatest asset in the journey of life. It is evident that everybody is looking for success, but spirituality is the key. This Ministry (David Oyedepo Ministries International) thrives absolutely by the Word and it is scaling new heights through the Word. In the same vein, Covenant and Landmark Universities are scaling new heights absolutely by the Word. Spirituality, therefore, remains our greatest asset in the journey of life. God spoke to me that in this end-time, saviours will rise from Mount Zion and this will only be realisable by the Word. As it is written:

And saviours shall come up on mount Zion to judge the mount of Esau; and the kingdom shall be the Lord's.

Obadiah 1:21

For instance, it is impossible to devour all the books of this Commission and not command enviable exploits. However, idleness, laziness, complacency and religiosity have hindered many from reaching their full potentials.

Friend, I read and devoured virtually all Kenneth Hagin and Kenneth Copeland's books. From 1976, God started preparing me for a great future and I accepted responsibility to get there. Most of my encounters in life came from those books.

When my wife and I were in courtship, our counsellor asked me, "What do you look forward to in your marriage?" I said, "Hitch-free marriage!" He said, "How do you mean?" I replied, "We have been in courtship for 5 years and everything is working fine." He said, "You see David, when you are far apart, it is difficult to step on one another's toes, but when you are living together, it is impossible not to step on one another's toes." I said to him humorously, "Sir, you and I are sitting on the same chair, why am I not stepping on your toes? One, I'm not blind. Two, I am not wicked." For all these years we have been married, we have never had a scuffle. That is the product of knowledge!

By spirituality, Joseph scaled utmost heights. A prisoner became the breadwinner of a nation. By spirituality, Daniel remained relevant to the government of Babylon for 65 years. By spirituality, Nehemiah rebuilt the walls of Jerusalem in 52 days. He fasted his way into favour.

A young man testified in one of our services that the company where he served as a Corps member had challenges and he told them that in Winners' Chapel, where he is a member, we engage the weapon of fasting to destroy barriers. Then he asked his manager, "Can we, therefore, fast in this company for three days?" The manager agreed; they all fasted for three days and there was a supernatural breakthrough. At the end of his service year, the company refused to release him because of the tremendous impact the young man made; so, he stayed for a few more years. Thereafter, he indicated his desire to go and was given an estate and Range Rover sports car to match. That's not long service award because the whole incident was less than four years; it is spirituality award. How can you, as a believer, have a company that is dying and you are sleeping? How can you Pastor a church that is not growing and you are sleeping? No wonder the Bible admonishes:

> *Wherefore he saith, Awake thou that sleepest ...*
> *and Christ shall give thee light.*
>
> *Ephesians 5:14*

We must, therefore, awake from our slumber and lay hold on the weapon of spirituality for fulfilment of our glorious destinies in Christ.

6

Think Like A Star

For as he thinketh in his heart, so is he ...

Proverbs 23:7

Nothing defines destiny like mentality. For our destinies to be actualised, we must possess possibility and success mentality.

> **And the LORD said, Behold, the people is one, and they have all one language; and this they begin to do: and now nothing will be restrained from them, which they have imagined to do.**
>
> *Genesis 11:6*

It is, therefore, possibility mentality that makes a giant. As it is written:

> **I can do all things through Christ which strengtheneth me.**
>
> *Philippians 4:13*

Until we change the way we think, it will be impossible

101

to change the way we live. The Bible says:

> *And be not conformed to this world: but be ye transformed by the renewing of your mind, that ye may prove what is that good, and acceptable, and perfect, will of God.*
>
> *Romans 12:2*

Proverbs 4:23 also says:

> *Keep thy heart with all diligence; for out of it are the issues of life.*

Our thoughts determine our lot in life. That is why it is failure mentality that makes a failure; lack mentality makes a pauper, and success mentality makes a star. It is our imagination that determines our destination.

> *Behold, the people is one, and they have all one language; and this they begin to do: and now nothing will be restrained from them, which they have imagined to do.*
>
> *Genesis 11:6*

It is a positive mentality that makes a giant. Therefore, our thoughts will either make us or break us.

> *For from within, out of the heart of men, proceed evil thoughts, adulteries, fornications, murders, Thefts, covetousness, wickedness, deceit, lasciviousness, an evil eye, blasphemy, pride, foolishness: All these*

evil things come from within, and defile the man.
                                              Mark 7:21-23

In essence, when great thoughts dominate our hearts, they result in our greatness. Naturally, evil thoughts bring about evil acts, and great thoughts empower us to take giant steps into greatness. Ultimately, our "thoughts" determines our destinies. The Bible says:

> *And be not conformed to this world: but be ye transformed by the renewing of your mind, that ye may prove what is that good, and acceptable, and perfect, will of God.*
>   *Romans 12:2*

In essence, until we change the way we think, we cannot change the way we live. Therefore, "Think like a Star." That is, cultivate the mentality of a star, because that is where stardom begins. It is also very important to recognise from James 1:21-25 that God's Word is the spiritual mirror that reveals our actual worth as children of God.

That means, we can catch our actual picture from the mirror of the Word. Also, in Proverbs 27:19, it is written: *As in water face answereth to face, so the heart of man to man*.

Furthermore, we are told that the Word of God is like water.

> *That he might sanctify and cleanse it with the*

washing of water by the word.

Ephesians 5:26

That means, God's Word is a bowl of water and every time we open the pages, the pictures of our destinies are revealed to us. For instance, in the mirror of the Word, every child of God is revealed as a lion. Why? Jesus is the Lion of the tribe of Judah and we are heirs of God, and joint-heirs with Him. The Bible records:

And one of the elders saith unto me, Weep not: behold, the Lion of the tribe of Juda, the Root of David, hath prevailed to open the book, and to loose the seven seals thereof. And I beheld, and, lo, in the midst of the throne and of the four beasts, and in the midst of the elders, stood a Lamb as it had been slain, having seven horns and seven eyes, which are the seven Spirits of God sent forth into all the earth.

Revelation 5:5-6

It is also written:

For both he that sanctifieth and they who are sanctified are all of one: for which cause he is not ashamed to call them brethren.

Hebrews 2:11

There is no way a sheep can be a brother to a lion. Thus, if God called us brethren, then we belong to the same class. If He is the Lion of the tribe of Judah, then, we belong to the lion's tribe; and that should make a difference in the way we think.

But, what makes a lion? Unusual strength that commands dominion.

It is written:

> **There be three things which go well, yea, four are comely in going: A lion which is strongest among beasts, and turneth not away for any.**
>
> *Proverbs 30:29-30*

We must understand that a lion's strength is not just in the physical but also within (inner strength), which translates to 'confidence'. The lion is not the biggest animal in the jungle; yet, it challenges other animals such as the elephant and the hippopotamus that are three times its size. This shows that it takes confidence to emerge a conqueror. For example, Joshua and Caleb were the youngest of the spies sent to Jericho, but they were super-confident in God. The lion in them came alive! Thus, the dominion of a lion is rooted in its confidence, and every child of God is redeemed a lion. As long as we remain sheep, we stand the risk of being slaughtered! Concerning Jesus, the Bible says:

> **He was oppressed, and he was afflicted, yet he opened not his mouth: he is brought as a lamb to the slaughter, and as a sheep before her shearers is dumb, so he openeth not his mouth.**
>
> *Isaiah 53:7*

By the revelation of the Word, we are eagles and lions, and, therefore the kings of the jungle and the kings of the air.

The truth is that we can't get what we cannot see. In the early years of Covenant University, I said, "There is no university we are trying to compete with in Nigeria. The ones that we are competing with are not here. A new generation Harvard is in the making." I could boldly declare these because I knew that no one arrives at a future he cannot see. The Bible says:

> *And the LORD said unto Abram, after that Lot was separated from him, Lift up now thine eyes, and look from the place where thou art northward, and southward, and eastward, and westward: For all the land which thou seest, to thee will I give it, and to thy seed for ever.*
>
> *Genesis 13:14-15*

Every child of God is a seed of Abraham; that means, we are Israelites indeed. That is why the Bible says:

> *And if ye be Christ's, then are ye Abraham's seed, and heirs according to the promise.*
>
> *Galatians 3:29*

Furthermore, it is written:

> *For he is not a Jew, which is one outwardly; neither is that circumcision, which is outward in the flesh: But*

he is a Jew, which is one inwardly; and circumcision is that of the heart, in the spirit, and not in the letter; whose praise is not of men, but of God.

Romans 2:28-29

Indeed, when we become born again, we are adopted as spiritual Jews. We must also understand that there are certain things we hear that we may not be able to believe. However, there are things we have seen that are difficult to doubt. The Bible says: *For we cannot but speak the things which we have seen and heard* (Acts 4:20).

That is why nobody can make us doubt what we have seen. Therefore, it is not enough to hear the Word of God and understand it, it is equally important for us to get pictures from the Scripture. It is written:

The word that Isaiah the son of Amoz saw concerning Judah and Jerusalem.

Isaiah 2:1

The truth is, many people have heard so many things, but they are yet to see anything. Therefore, we must move from revelations to the visions of the Lord, which are contained in His Book, and nothing creates a future like being able to see them.

Concerning His identity on earth, Jesus said:

I Jesus have sent mine angel to testify unto you these things in the churches. I am the root and the

offspring of David, and the bright and morning star.
Revelation 22:16

Thus, if Jesus came to earth as a star, then there is a star in us because He said: *...as my Father hath sent me, even so send I you* (John 20:21).

Our destinies are loaded. Beyond that, the Bible says:

For the LORD God is a sun and shield: the LORD will give grace and glory: no good thing will he withhold from them that walk uprightly.
Psalm 84:11

Moreover, Jesus is the Sun of Righteousness with healing in his wings.

For, behold, the day cometh, that shall burn as an oven; and all the proud, yea, and all that do wickedly, shall be stubble: and the day that cometh shall burn them up, saith the LORD of hosts, that it shall leave them neither root nor branch. But unto you that fear my name shall the Sun of righteousness arise with healing in his wings; and ye shall go forth, and grow up as calves of the stall.
Malachi 4:1-2

Now, what do these scriptures mean? All fountains of life, mysteriously, draw from the sun. That is why the Bible says:

And of Zion it shall be said, This and that man was born in her: and the highest himself shall establish her. The LORD shall count, when he writeth up the people, that this man was born there. As well the singers as the players on instruments shall be there: all my springs are in thee.

Psalm 87:5-7

Thus, we are assets to our world, not liabilities. We are fountains of life to our generation, not concerns. Remember, *there is one glory of the sun, another glory of the moon and another glory of the stars: for one star differeth from another star in glory* (1 Corinthians 15:41).

We have been talking about stars rising, but very soon, we shall be seeing the "suns" rise! Our sun will shine and multitudes will draw life from us. We will never be sources of concern to anyone, any day of our lives! Wherever we are found, life will be oozing forth! The Bible is filled with God's visions for us; therefore, it is time to start thinking right! As it is written:

Finally, brethren, whatsoever things are true, whatsoever things are honest, whatsoever things are just, whatsoever things are pure, whatsoever things are lovely, whatsoever things are of good report; if there be any virtue, and if there be any praise, think on these things.

Philippians 4:8

This is God's curriculum for our thought pattern. We carry amazing treasures; our lives must not end as trash.

Now, let's take a closer look at the things that are very familiar. God told Abraham after he was called:

> *...I will make of thee a great nation, and I will bless thee, and make thy name great; and thou shalt be a blessing: And I will bless them that bless thee, and curse him that curseth thee: and in thee shall all families of the earth be blessed.*
>
> *Genesis 12:2-3*

We must recognise that Jesus died to connect us to the Abrahamic order of blessings. The Bible records:

> *Christ hath redeemed us from the curse of the law, being made a curse for us: for it is written, Cursed is every one that hangeth on a tree: That the blessing of Abraham might come on the Gentiles through Jesus Christ; that we might receive the promise of the Spirit through faith.*
>
> *Galatians 3:13-14*

Consequently, we are not just Nigerians, Africans, Britons or Americans, but global citizens! God also said to Abraham:

> *And in thy seed shall all the nations of the earth be blessed; because thou hast obeyed my voice.*
>
> *Genesis 22:18*

Hence, God has ordained us to be sources of blessing to all the families of the earth. I am not referring to the success of having what to eat, drink, get married, have children, get old and eventually say farewell to this world. No! I am talking about leaving indelible marks for upcoming generations. I am referring to things that will be happening hundred years after we are gone.

Therefore, it is time to renew our minds with the truth, so that we can experience amazing transformations in our journeys. The truth is, we will never shine brighter or be greater than our thoughts. Everything about our tomorrow is determined by our thoughts today.

The Bible says:

> *For a good tree bringeth not forth corrupt fruit; neither doth a corrupt tree bring forth good fruit. For every tree is known by his own fruit. For of thorns men do not gather figs, nor of a bramble bush gather they grapes. A good man out of the good treasure of his heart bringeth forth that which is good; and an evil man out of the evil treasure of his heart bringeth forth that which is evil: for of the abundance of the heart his mouth speaketh.*
>
> Luke 6:43-45

Our thoughts determine the fruits we bear. We cannot sow tomato seed and expect to harvest maize. Every good tree brings forth good fruit and every evil tree brings forth evil fruits. This simply means that evil thoughts produce evil acts, and every great thought breeds great results. That is why we are advised: *keep thy heart with all diligence; for out of it are the issues of life.* Proverbs 4:23

I have said over and again, "I am not surprised at where we are today – thank God for it, because He made it happen; but, I would have been surprised if we are not here." I carry the love for the entire world in my heart. I had no personal dream for personal comfort. My entire dream is, "Who can be helped next?" or "Who requires a smile on his face?"

After we built our house in Lagos, one of my sons came in from the mission field and said, "This must be a dream come true!" I said, "I never dreamt about this!" The truth is that I never had the time to even check the drawing. That is not where my thought is. Also, during the building of the church office, all the drawings were on my table but I never had the opportunity to check them once. However, I was busy checking for who would come to church next, what he/she would need and how God would meet his/her needs. At that time, they had built the office complex to the top, but I couldn't get there earlier, though I was living in the vicinity. It was when the building was completed that I was shown my office. No doubt, our thoughts today determine our heights tomorrow!

Many years ago, I went to Jos (a city in the Middle Belt area of Nigeria) to see the Corp members posted to our Mission. As I drove off that place, I saw a plain land and said, "This will be nice for the university we are going to build." I was in a Volkswagen beetle, but I already saw a university. Presently, our Church has two universities. Don't think trials; think testimonies. Don't think defeat; think conquest. It is written:

> *According as his divine power hath given unto us all things that pertain unto life and godliness, through the knowledge of him that hath called us to glory and virtue.*
>
> *2 Peter 1:3*

Whatever we need in this world is contained in the Bible, but they are delivered through the knowledge of Christ. Thus, when we think in line with God's thoughts, we are on the way to unbelievable heights. As the Lord lives, that is where we are going!

God said:

> *For my thoughts are not your thoughts, neither are your ways my ways, saith the LORD. For as the heavens are higher than the earth, so are my ways higher than your ways, and my thoughts than your thoughts*
>
> *Isaiah 55:8-9*

God's thoughts and ways are in His Words. One day, I saw clearly that indebtedness is not part of redemption. God told me that it is impossible to serve two masters.

You will have to choose one and despise the other, and the borrower is a servant to the lender. Therefore, I chose the God of heaven as against any lender in the world. Till date, not one dime has been borrowed from anywhere in the world to run the ministry.

One day, I saw from the Word that God is no respecter of persons, but in any nation – including Nigeria, anyone that fears God and works according to His rule will command the same order of result. Thus, there is nothing anywhere in the world for me to envy. No! We have equal access to heaven.

For there is no difference between the Jew and the Greek: for the same Lord over all is rich unto all that call upon him.

Romans 10:12

I read a book many years ago titled, *The Power of Positive Thinking* by Norman Vincent Peale. It connected me to another realm and changed my entire concept of redemption forever. I learnt from there that we can determine the events of our lives by the thoughts of our hearts. Therefore, we must spend time investing in our lives, what we want to see in our future.

The Bible is full of revelations but very importantly, of visions. The Bible reveals to us what we are made of, what we are worth and the treasures hidden in us. However, we must understand that until we can see these treasures, we are not set to have them. From today, may our eyes begin to see very clearly every picture painted of us in the Scripture! It will settle us for life! We cannot afford to disappoint destiny because everything we need to live impactful lives are available to us in Christ. I wrote something sometimes ago that I called the 'Star's Creed'. It is like a Psalm. You can also call it the 'Psalm of Stars'. It is about what and how we think. It goes thus:

Psalm of Stars

I am not disadvantaged: Many people think because they are black, they are backward; because they are Africans, they have no worth. Although I am black, I am not disadvantaged; I am not underprivileged. I am not unfortunate; I am not unlucky. I am just in shape for the topmost top in life.

I am not oppressed; I am not depressed. I am not afflicted. I am anointed a king to reign on the earth.

I am not failing; I am not losing. I am not begging; I am giving, winning and gaining.

I am the light of the world. I am the salt of the earth. I am a city set upon a hill that cannot be hidden. I surely have something to offer my world. You are not a beggarly citizen of the earth. It is high time you started thinking so.

I am peculiar; I am treasure-loaded. I am unique; I have the mind of Christ. I surely have what it takes to impact my world. We mustn't pass through the earth unnoticed, not because we are hunting for fame, but by reason of the value we will add wherever we are found.

I am not drowning, and I am not sinking; I am a burning and shining light. Anybody who plays around me has signed for his doom.

I am not a burden; I am not a concern. I am not a reproach; I am created for the envy of my world. I am indeed a blessing to my generation.

Sometimes ago, a woman came to my office and I said, "I taught this girl in 1977." Some pastors were there with me and I asked her, "Please, tell them Theresa, was I a good teacher?" She said, "You are teaching the Church with the same passion you taught us."

We have something to offer our world. Therefore, let's think "the world" and not just our pockets, title or status. If we think impact, it will determine where we find ourselves ultimately. This approach to life will help us to be disciplined.

A wise person said, "Sow a thought and you reap an act. Sow an act and you reap a habit. Sow a habit, you reap a character. Sow a character and you reap a destiny." Thus, everything about our destinies begins with a thought.

In 1970, I found in my Bible that we have been redeemed unto our God as priests and kings. *And hast made us unto our God kings and priests: and we shall reign on the earth* (Revelation 5:10). It, then, occurred to me that I don't have to belong to a royal family on the earth to be regarded as royalty; and that being redeemed connects me to heavenly royalty and it must reflect on the earth.

That immediately affected the way I dressed. I would ask myself, "Will a king go out like this?" Nobody preached this to me, I discovered it myself. Whenever I was provoked for any reason, instead of shouting, I would tell myself, "A king wouldn't shout on the street."

At this moment, I will like you to pray: "Lord, help me to go beyond hearing to seeing the picture You have painted for me in Your Book." That is the picture of confidence in God and the picture of clear direction on the pathway to follow. It is written:

> *For who hath known the mind of the Lord, that he may instruct him? But we have the mind of Christ.*
>
> 1 Corinthians 2:16

That means, we can never be listed among failures

because the excellent spirit of Christ is in us. Can you imagine that? The mind that created the entire world is in us. This is not religious talk; it is God's direct vision of us. When we got saved, He brought us into a mind transplant theatre and replaced our human minds with the Creator's mind. So, we are a peculiar people and our case is different. We have what it takes to change our world and create the world we want to live in. God will be raising men like nations in this end-time. I see us being a part of it! Therefore, a great tomorrow awaits you! A great future awaits you! You will live a great life! You will be a blessing to all those around you! Everything about your life will be working perfectly and in order, in Jesus' name!

7

Let The Eagle Soar!

Ye are the salt of the earth: but if the salt have lost his savour, wherewith shall it be salted? It is thenceforth good for nothing, but to be cast out, and to be trodden under foot of men. Ye are the light of the world. A city that is set on an hill cannot be hid. Neither do men light a candle, and put it under a bushel, but on a candlestick; and it giveth light unto all that are in the house. Let your light so shine before men, that they may see your good works, and glorify your Father which is in heaven.

Matthew 5:13-16

Although we are eagles, we must allow the eagle in us to soar or it will become a mere accolade. We must also recognise that being the light of the world does not guarantee our shining. The opening scripture says, **"...Let your light so shine..."** Therefore, making it shine is our responsibility! Our light does not shine because God has made us lights; rather, it is what we make of that light that determines how much it shines. Remember that we are eagles by redemption because like begets like, and everything produces after its kind. For instance, a cow will not give birth to a lamb; neither will a lamb give birth to a dog. It is written:

> *Ye have seen what I did unto the Egyptians, and how I bare you on eagles' wings, and brought you unto myself.*
>
> *Exodus 19:4*

The consciousness of who we are determines what we dare. God said to Moses:

> *Come now therefore, and I will send thee unto Pharaoh, that thou mayest bring forth my people the children of Israel out of Egypt.*
>
> *Exodus 3:10*

Hence, Moses was the eagle through whom God delivered the Israelites.

> *And by a prophet the LORD brought Israel out of Egypt, and by a prophet was he preserved.*
>
> *Hosea 12:13*

It is also written:

> *For Moses truly said unto the fathers, A prophet shall the Lord your God raise up unto you of your brethren, like unto me; him shall ye hear in all things whatsoever he shall say unto you.*
>
> *Acts 3:22*

In the above scripture, Moses was futuristically referring to Jesus. Thus, Jesus came as an eagle and He said: *As my Father hath sent me, even so send I you* (John 20:21).

Therefore, we need to know that we are eagles, because that is what determines what we will ever dare. The consciousness of who we are is important in the race of life. We must understand that as eagles, we are not meant to fly, but soar. Therefore, I decree your soaring now!

When Moses appeared in Egypt, everyone was looking at him in the "sky" because he was unstoppable and irresistible! He arrived and said, "Let my people go" and that was it. Similarly, when Jesus, being a carpenter's son, began to manifest His eagle nature, the Bible says that all eyes were fixed on Him and His fame went abroad suddenly.

Catch a Vision and Run With It

It is very important to recognise that no aircraft is allowed to fly without a defined destination. That is, before a plane is allowed to take off, the control tower must have the details of where it is going and the route it will fly to get there. That is what we call vision and dream. A vision gave birth to the eagle-Moses and a vision brought forth the eagle-Christ.

It is impossible for anyone to soar without a vision of where he is headed to. The Bible says:

> *Where there is no vision, the people perish: but he that keepeth the law, happy is he.*
>
> *Proverbs 29:18*

Jesus knew what He came to do on earth, He knew how to go about it and He knew when He finished it. It is written:

> *The Spirit of the Lord is upon me, because he hath anointed me to preach the gospel to the poor; he hath sent me to heal the brokenhearted, to preach deliverance to the captives, and recovering of sight to the blind, to set at liberty them that are bruised, To preach the acceptable year of the Lord.*
>
> *Luke 4:18-19*

> *...For this purpose the Son of God was manifested, that he might destroy the works of the devil.*
>
> *1 John 3:8*

> *...When Jesus therefore had received the vinegar, he said, It is finished: and he bowed his head, and gave up the ghost.*
>
> *John 19:30*

Furthermore, God said:

> *Before I formed thee in the belly I knew thee; and before thou camest forth out of the womb I sanctified thee, and I ordained thee a prophet*

unto the nations.

Jeremiah 1:5

We are on the earth for a particular mission and a discovery of that mission is called vision or dream. That is where we are programmed to go and that is where we will be engraced to manifest. Therefore, it is so important to know and place appropriate values on the power of dreams.

And it shall come to pass afterward, that I will pour out my spirit upon all flesh; and your sons and your daughters shall prophesy, your old men shall dream dreams, your young men shall see visions:

Joel 2:28

The ministry of the Holy Spirit is to unfold God's plan as it relates to each one on earth. He is to receive from the Lord and show it to us.

Howbeit when he, the Spirit of truth, is come, he will guide you into all truth: for he shall not speak of himself; but whatsoever he shall hear, that shall he speak: and he will shew you things to come.

John 16:13

It is, therefore, important to know that God has a plan and a discovery of that plan empowers the eagle in us to soar. May we not miss that great plan and purpose of God for our lives! That is what the eagle in us is waiting for to soar. That is what the control tower in heaven is waiting for, to allow us take-off in the air. Our destination must be properly defined before we are allowed to fly.

Joseph was in prison the previous night, and the following morning, he became a Prime Minister. That is the power of dreams! He knew where he was going; therefore, all the things that accompany dreams were evident in his life. We cannot have genuine dreams without passion, self-discipline and crave for the wisdom to actualise our dreams. We saw in Joseph, self-discipline, diligence and wisdom. These are all companions of a genuine dream. People live carelessly because they have dreamless/visionless lives. Joseph said:

> ...*how then can I do this great wickedness, and sin against God?*
>
> *Genesis 39:9*

Self-discipline was his companion because he carried a genuine dream in his heart. He was living in the excitement of his future. We cannot have a dream of tomorrow and not begin to live in the reality of it today by our dispositions. In this context, a dream is a mental picture or formation of our future, of which we are fully persuaded. That persuasion expresses itself in passion, self-discipline, diligence and wisdom.

For the eagle in us to come alive, we must commit to discovering our mission on earth by asking God to reveal it to us.

The Word says:

> *For I know the thoughts that I think toward you, saith the LORD, thoughts of peace, and not of evil, to give you an expected end. Then shall ye call upon me, and ye shall go and pray unto me, and I will hearken unto you. And ye shall seek me, and find me, when ye shall search for me with all your heart.*
>
> *Jeremiah 29:11-13*

That means, "Come for My plans for you, if you are interested. Seek Me with all your heart and I will deliver it to you, and give colour to your life." There is no product in the market without a particular function. In the same vein, there is no one on earth without a purpose in the heart of God concerning him. We are not biological accidents; rather, we are definite creatures of a definite God. He has a purpose on the earth for us; all we need to do is settle down and discover it on time because He only makes all things beautiful in His time.

We have the responsibility to define our destinations in our youthful days, so that we can have enough time to pursue and deliver the details of our mandates. Joseph caught a vision at the age of 17; and at the age of 30, he was Prime Minister in Egypt. David confronted Goliath at the age of 17; then, he became a king in Israel at the age of 30. Jesus found where it was written of Him at the age of 30; thereafter, He erupted and the world is yet to recover from His impact. This is your time and chance; don't mess it up!

Too many people in the body of Christ are merely surviving; very few are truly impacting. We are not created to survive; we are created to impact. That is why the Bible says that we are the light of the world, the salt of the earth and cities set on hills that cannot be hidden. Therefore, we are not on earth for mere survival but for impact and exploits.

Always remember that no aircraft is allowed to take off without its destination properly defined. In the same vein, no believer will ever soar without his vision properly defined. This is because it is the detailed revelation of our destinations that qualifies us to soar.

What Are the Key Characteristics of an Eagle?

The Eagle Possesses Extraordinary Strength

...the people that do know their God shall be strong, and do exploits.

Daniel 11:32

The eagle is a very strong bird and it takes strength to do exploit. It can pick up any prey three times its own weight – a man, goat, ram, etc, and that is the Spirit of might. Men and women of exploits require strength.

A global impact will make global demands on our lives. Therefore, we need a new order of strength to emerge as men and women of exploits. Receive the outpouring of the Spirit of might, in Jesus' name!

When we sow sparingly, we reap sparingly; but when we invest bountifully, we reap bountifully. I have kept a work pace of nothing less than 16 hours a day for many years. So, don't say, "He must be very lucky." Our impact will never outgrow our input, and we need strength, via the Spirit of might, to enhance our input.

In 1981, I was reading one of the biographies of John Wesley and I saw him in a cross-country horseback ride for the gospel at the age of 80. That testimony imparted strength to my system. I received the impartation of the Spirit of might while reading that biography.

We must understand that the reason we read is not just to be informed, but also to be imparted by the spirits of men and women who have gone ahead of us. I have never had a breakdown and I cannot have one. I want to believe that it is wrong work that wears people out, not right work or hard work. By the time you go gossiping all over town, you will be weary. When you start collecting data about everybody, you will be tired. When you start speaking valueless words, you will be gone. However, when we get on key with our own assignment, we go from strength to strength, not from weakness to weakness.

> *Wherefore lift up the hands which hang down, and the feeble knees; And make straight paths for your feet, lest that which is lame be turned out of the way; but let it rather be healed.*
>
> *Hebrews 12:12-13*

I decree a fresh impartation of the Spirit of might upon your life!

You might say, "Where is the place of the anointing, if I have to work so hard?" Jesus, the most anointed man that walked on planet earth, said, *I must work the works of him that sent me, while it is day: the night cometh, when no man can work* (John 9:4).

He further said in John 5:17: *My Father worketh hitherto and I work*. Also, after ministering to the Samaritan woman by the well, He said to His disciples, I have some food to eat that you don't know about.

> *...My meat is to do the will of him that sent me, and to finish his work.*
>
> *John 4:34*

To enhance our worth, work is a must. Whatever we

don't earn will never add value to us. Wealth gotten by vanity shall diminish. Whatever gift our father or mother gives us will not enhance our worth; but he that gathers by labour shall increase. Therefore, receive grace to be a productive worker and labourer, in the name of Jesus!

Paul, a man of unusual revelation, said:

> **But by the grace of God I am what I am: and his grace which was bestowed upon me was not in vain; but I laboured more abundantly than they all: yet not I, but the grace of God which was with me.**
>
> *1 Corinthians 15:10*

Our level of labour defines the beauty of our future; there is no shortcut. If we are not workers, our worth will not be enhanced and we will end up as beggars and liabilities. Therefore, an extra input in our studies, businesses, careers, etc, with faith in God, will take us to enviable heights. Remember, there is nothing extraordinary on its own; it is man's extraordinary input that makes it so. Thus, we must work for the eagle in us to fully emerge and manifest.

Moreover, it is vital to recognise that revelation is one of the vital keys to accessing divine strength.

> **A wise man is strong; yea, a man of knowledge increaseth strength.**
>
> *Proverbs 24:5*

But they that wait upon the LORD shall renew their strength; they shall mount up with wings as eagles; they shall run, and not be weary; and they shall walk, and not faint.

Isaiah 40:31

Just like the eagle, let us suck water from the rock and honey from where it is available before we take to the sky.

The Eagle is a Bird with Very Strong Character

It is so important to know that one of the key characteristics of the eagle is moral strength. Joseph was a man of strong character. The Bible says:

There is none greater in this house than I; neither hath he kept back any thing from me but thee, because thou art his wife: how then can I do this great wickedness, and sin against God?

Genesis 39:9

Usually, when we talk about strength, we think only of physical abilities, but that does not weigh much in the school of exploits. We are talking about emotional and moral strength. We must be emotionally stable with great moral strength.

Every eagle that will truly soar must have a strong character. For instance, Job feared God and eschewed evil, and he became the greatest of all men in his days.

He had a very strong character.

And the LORD said unto Satan, Hast thou considered my servant Job, that there is none like him in the earth, a perfect and an upright man, one that feareth God, and escheweth evil?

Job 1:8

When Job's wife advised him to curse God, he shut her up, because to him, she was speaking like one of the foolish women. Job said with confidence, *Though He slay me, yet will I trust in Him* (Job 13:15). Abraham told the King of Sodom that he would not take anything from him lest he boasted of making him rich.

My wife and I were in courtship for 6 years. One day, the devil said, "I will make you crash by fornication." I said, "Lord, if I dare it, smite me with leprosy." If we do not portray godly character, we don't have a future.

The test of a real eagle is inner strength.

That he would grant you, according to the riches of his glory, to be strengthened with might by his Spirit in the inner man.

Ephesians 3:16

It is impossible to command exploits without spiritual, moral and emotional strength. The eagle takes time to build that strength; it does not assume it. Let us understand that there is no special gospel for any group; it is one gospel for all people. If we don't inculcate our children with the raw gospel, they will become rotten. If you play with your life today, you will pay for it tomorrow.

The Eagle is a Highly Disciplined Bird

Annually, the eagle waits for about 40 days on the mountain, sheds old feathers, grows new ones and is set to soar for the next one year. When the Eagle-Jesus came, He fasted for 40 days. When the Eagle-Moses came, he also was in a fast for 40 days. Therefore, we need high-level spiritual discipline for the eagle in us to emerge, because every great story is traceable to high-level discipline. Receive grace for high-level discipline, in the name of Jesus! From today, nothing dislodges your destiny or overthrows you! Everything that God has ordained for you will be fulfilled in your life, in the name of Jesus Christ!

Eagles don't flock, they soar

Look unto Abraham your father, and unto Sarah that bare you: for I called him alone, and blessed him, and increased him. For the Lord shall comfort Zion: he will comfort all her waste places; and he will make her wilderness like Eden, and her desert like the garden of the Lord; joy and gladness shall be found therein, thanksgiving, and the voice of melody.
Isaiah 51:2-3

We must accept full responsibility for the outcome of our lives. We must not be foolish enough to let somebody else derail our destinies. We have nobody to blame for where our lives finally end. *Look to Abraham your father and to Sarah that bear thee, I called him alone and I blessed him* (Isaiah 51:2).

God has not changed; He still relates with us on individual basis! It is written:

> *And, behold, I come quickly; and my reward is with me, to give every man according as his work shall be.*
>
> *Revelation 22:12*

We must understand that God does not bless groups; He blesses individuals. He does not lift groups; he lifts individuals. He does not enlarge groups; He enlarges individuals.

In my spiritual journey from 1969 till date, my friends are either on fire for God like me or we remain acquaintances. I fasted my way out of the crowd; I prayed my way out of the general run, and I searched my way into unfathomable heights. There was no guesswork or assumption. I started my own spiritual library at the age of 20. I have read a few things and found God on many pages.

We must wake up and take full responsibility for

the outcome of our lives. Our parents do not have any business with where our future ends; we have the responsibility. We can only be taught which way to go; but we are the ones who take the responsibility to get there.

No aircraft tows another in the air. Everything that flies generates the power within itself to fly. Vehicles are towed on the road, ships on the sea, but not an aircraft. There is what is called ground-power. Every aircraft must generate adequate ground-power to make an upthrust and break through the barriers of gravity to remain in the sky.

How much ground-power we generate determines how high we fly. Have you ever watched a rocket taking off? It is not smoke but fire that is released because of the distance it will cover. Therefore, how much ground-power we succeed in generating determines the level of heights we will ever scale.

However, there are different power levels. The helicopter flies at a height that will enable it to see everybody as it goes; it can't go higher than that. Then, there is the propeller engine aircraft; it also flies at certain heights. We also have the proper jet, which reaches 40 or 50 thousand feet above sea level; you cannot see anything, except the sky. Then, we talk about the rockets. They are all separately powered and they carry different costs.

The eagle in some people may never soar because they have not generated what it takes to get to the sky. Some will get to the helicopter level, others to the propeller engine level and some others to the jet range. There is no shortcut; we are either ready for it or not!

Our picture as eagles has been properly painted from the Scripture and the multifaceted anointing we need for the eagle in us to manifest has also been released. I, therefore, decree that by your encounter from this book, you will no longer be found at the low level of life!

An Eagle is a Creature of Swiftness/Speed

David was lamenting the death of Saul and Jonathan when he said:

> **Saul and Jonathan were lovely and pleasant in their lives, and in their death they were not divided: they were swifter than eagles, they were stronger than lions.**
> *2 Samuel 1:23*

It is also written:

> **The LORD shall bring a nation against thee from far, from the end of the earth, as swift as the eagle flieth; a nation whose tongue thou shalt not understand.**
> *Deuteronomy 28:49*

This is God using the swiftness of an eagle as an analogy. As it is commonly said: "As swift as an eagle."

An eagle is a creature of unique speed. It doesn't just fly, it dives. An eagle dives into the sea to pick fishes and hardly misses its target.

In three-and-a-half years, Jesus took the world by storm and we are yet to recover from the impact of His mission. He imparted all generations of humanity yet unborn. He accomplished unusual feats with unique speed. Divine speed is one of the manifestations of the eagle in us. I see you experiencing divine speed!

It Takes Advantage of the Direction of the Wind for Its Flight

This is one of the features of the Eagle that ensures it does not struggle or sweat like other birds. The Eagle perches on the mountaintop, or the branch of a very tall tree, and watches out for the wind going in its direction; then it spreads its wings for the wind to carry it. The Eagle does not flap its wings to fly; rather, it soars by the direction of the wind. The eagle is a visionary bird; it operates by the direction of the wind. Thus, while other birds are flying against the direction of the wind, the eagle is just taking advantage of the wind and soaring towards uttermost heights.

One of the symbols of the Holy Spirit in Scripture is wind. Thus, just as the eagle experiences ease, as it soars by the direction of the wind, we experience stress-free journey in life, when we are led by the Holy Spirit. We are simply being carried by the wind.

> *For as many as are led by the Spirit of God, they are the sons of God.*
>
> Romans 8:14

Remember the Bible says:

> *And it shall come to pass afterward, that I will pour out my spirit upon all flesh; and your sons and your daughters shall prophesy, your old men shall dream dreams, your young men shall see visions.*
>
> Joel 2:28

I have explained this before: the Holy Spirit goes before us, He goes with us, He works with us, He works through us and works for us, when we are led by Him. We are just being carried. That is why those who are led by the Holy Spirit don't sweat to get results. You won't miss God's plan for your life anymore! I decree clarity of vision for your life! Your life will not be squandered! You shall not miss your place in destiny, in Jesus' name!

On the Day of Pentecost, the Holy Ghost came as a mighty rushing wind. Thus, every time we are led by the Holy Spirit, we are carried by the wind of God to His defined purpose for our lives. If you study the ministry of Moses, you will discover this profound statement reoccurring: *And the Lord said unto Moses.* That means everything Moses did, God instructed him to do it.

At the arrival of Jesus, our exemplary Eagle, He said, **"I can of mine own self do nothing: as I hear, I judge"** (John 5:30). That's what makes an eagle; it does not struggle like other birds because it takes advantage of the direction of the wind to soar. That is what makes it different.

Everywhere the Spirit of God leads us is a place of dignity and honour. It is not enough to know our destination; we must know the step by step details of how to get there; that is what the eagle does. It does not only build strength, it watches the direction of the wind to determine where it goes.

> *And Joseph was thirty years old when he stood before Pharaoh king of Egypt. And Joseph went out from the presence of Pharaoh, and went throughout all the land of Egypt.*
>
> *Genesis 41:46*

Joseph was 30 years when he "took off in the sky", the challenges notwithstanding. I don't care what you are going through; you will soon be found in the "sky"!

> *David was thirty years old when he began to reign, and he reigned forty years.*
>
> *2 Samuel 5:4*

All these men were young fellows who caught the direction of God for their lives on time. What took others decades to accomplish, like the speed of an eagle, you will get it done in a year!

> **And Jesus himself began to be about thirty years of age, being (as was supposed) the son of Joseph, which was the son of Heli.**
>
> *Luke 3:23*

You may not hear a voice, but there is a passion inside you; that is a pointer to God's mission for your life. There is something you wish could be better than what it is right now; in most cases, that is a pointer to God's assignment for your life.

> **For it is God which worketh in you both to will and to do of his good pleasure.**
>
> *Philippians 2:13*

Therefore, every positive passion should have your attention. Unfortunately, in today's world, what people call passion is nothing but an obsession, because they want something out of it. Your assignment is not about what to get, it is about what to give. It is not about what you have, but what to do. Today, what people call vision is to become a doctor. When you ask them the reason for their choice, they say they want a name and a title. That is not a vision.

Nehemiah never thought of becoming a governor; he was just burdened with passion to see the broken walls built. He was a chief labourer in the building of the wall and had no dream of becoming a leader. He was only a passionate builder of the broken wall, to restore the glory of Jerusalem.

David never thought of becoming a king; he just couldn't stand the name of the Lord being assaulted by Goliath. He said, "Let me die the death of the righteous than watch this continue." It was a passion for God and His people that drove him, not a passion for himself. Living for self is what makes a slave; living for others is what makes a leader. Your assignment is what will define your attainment in life.

We went to Indonesia and one of the top businessmen there said to me, "Why don't you become the President of Nigeria?" I replied that it is not my assignment. My assignment is so defined that nothing else would ever hold an attraction for me till I die.

Some fellows met Billy Graham and said, "We will sponsor your presidency for this nation." He replied that it was not God's plan for him. Some other fellows said they would build a university in his name and he said that was not God's plan for him. God's plan for him is simply to preach the gospel to all nations. He is over 90 years and still relevant. It is not about any attainment or entitlement; it is about your assignment.

Mother Teresa cared for all the poor people in India and sacrificed for them. In her lifetime, she was given a standing ovation at the United Nations' General

Assembly. It is not what we have that determines our worth, but what we add to the human race. What service are you to render? May you find your place on time!

Every godly passion in you is a pointer to your mission on earth. You may never hear a voice from heaven, but by divine order, that mission can be conveyed to you through a godly passion to add value to the human race.

I will like us to see these compendiums of visions:

By vision, Abraham soared in the sky. The Bible says:

Now the LORD had said unto Abram, Get thee out of thy country, and from thy kindred, and from thy father's house, unto a land that I will shew thee: And I will make of thee a great nation, and I will bless thee, and make thy name great; and thou shalt be a blessing:

Genesis 12:1-2

That was an encounter with God. Moses also had an encounter with God at the burning bush. Paul had an encounter with God on his way to Damascus and a great Apostle emerged.

Think of what dream or passion delivers. It was said of Joseph: **Behold this dreamer cometh** (Genesis 37:19).

David declared

...for who is this uncircumcised Philistine, that he

should defy the armies of the living God? David said moreover, The LORD that delivered me out of the paw of the lion, and out of the paw of the bear, he will deliver me out of the hand of this Philistine...
1 Samuel 17:26, 37

That is a dream expressed in passion.

Nehemiah was passionate about rebuilding the wall of Jerusalem. It was an expression of the dream in his heart. This is to help us understand that visions, dreams and passions deliver at the same level and quality. See where vision took Abraham and where dreams took Joseph. See where vision took Moses and where a dream took David. They all had the same source, that is, God.

The young men, as earlier seen in Joel 2:28, are designed to see visions and have great dreams. God never said to me that Covenant University shall be a new generation Harvard; it was a dream of my heart. That is the kind of quality we look forward to generating and the value we are out to discharge. Therefore, without a vision or a dream, destiny is doomed. We do not have a future without a dream or vision. Hence, we need to catch a dream, in order not to be doomed.

Most times, God's great plans are unfolded in ordinary times. Moses was rearing his father-in-law's sheep when he suddenly received a signal. That is why a carnal man ends up a loser and his life ends in regrets;

the day God speaks, he may not be there. I pray that, from this day, living in the Spirit will become a natural lifestyle for you! It was an ordinary day when David took food to the warfront for his brothers and, then, destiny answered. It was an ordinary day for Gideon when an angel appeared to him. May that ordinary day that conveys your assignment on earth not be lost to carnality!

One of the greatest trainings in the world is how to walk in the Spirit, because that is what connects us to God on a 24-hour basis. When we are connected to God, we cannot be frustrated on the earth. It was on an ordinary day that the Liberation Mandate was delivered to me. I was in my bathroom when the mandate for Lagos was delivered; I was not praying. I was driving from Lagos to Kaduna on an ordinary day when the mandate for Africa was delivered.

> *I was in the Spirit on the Lord's day, and heard*
> *behind me a great voice, as of a trumpet.*
> *Revelation 1:10*

You do not hear because you are not in the Spirit. You are plagued with a lot of junk thoughts, frivolous browsing and non-beneficial news from the television. Most profound events in the world take place on ordinary days. Receive the grace to walk in the Spirit as a lifestyle, in the name of Jesus!

The Bible says that an army is rising and there has never been the kind of them, neither would there be any like them until the years of many generations. Behind them is a desolate wilderness and nothing shall escape them (Joel 2:2-8). That is dominion. What is it that distinguishes them? Vision!

When we walk in God's ways, He gets the job done. You will not miss your step all the days of your life! All the 'eagles' we saw in the Scripture had their root in visions and revelations. They got on key with divine plan for the eagle in them to soar. I decree that any plan of the devil to get you trapped is broken today, in the name of Jesus! You shall not miss the leading of the Lord all the days of your life! Receive the grace to soar like the eagle that God has made you, in Jesus' name! See you at the top!

ABOUT THE *Author*

David O. Oyedepo, called to be an Apostle with a mandate to liberate the world through the preaching of the Word of Faith, has for nearly four decades been part of the ongoing charismatic revival sweeping across the African continent today. His faith-based teachings have literarily transformed millions of lives around the world.

He is the Founder and President of the Living Faith Church Worldwide also known as Winners' Chapel International, with a network of thousands of Churches in Nigeria and several other nations across the continents of the world.

Till date, he has published over 90 impactful titles most of which have been translated to major languages of the world such as French, Chinese, Spanish etc. with over twenty million copies in circulation.

He is the Senior Pastor of the Faith Tabernacle, Canaanland, Ota, Nigeria, with a 50,000-seat sanctuary, reputed to be the largest church facility in the world. The church currently runs five services on Sunday morning with over 300,000 worshippers, making her one of the largest church congregations in the world.

His mission has established educational institutions across all levels in Nigeria, with Covenant and Landmark Universities taking large strides towards becoming world class universities.

He is married to Faith and they are blessed with sons, daughters and grandchildren.

Books By Dr David Oyedepo

- Following The Path Of The Eagle
- The Exceeding Riches Of His Grace
- Not By Power Nor By Might
- The Turnaround Power Of The Word
- Understanding The Power Of Faith
- The Breakthrough Power Of Vision
- On Eagle's Wings
- The Unlimited Power Of Faith
- In Pursuit Of Vision
- Pillars Of Destiny
- Signs & Wonders Today
- Exploits In Ministry
- Winning The War Against Poverty
- Walking In Dominion
- Possessing Your Possession
- The Wisdom That Works
- Exploits Of Faith
- Anointing For Exploits
- Understanding The Power Of Praise
- Walking In Newness Of Life
- Maximise Destiny
- Commanding The Supernatural
- Winning Invisible Battles
- Success Systems
- Understanding Financial Prosperity
- Success Strategies
- Understanding Your Covenant Right
- Miracle Meal
- Exploring the Riches of Redemption
- Anointing For Breakthrough
- Excellency Of Wisdom
- Breaking Financial Hardship
- The Release Of Power
- Walking In The Miraculous

Books By Dr David Oyedepo

- Satan Get Lost!
- The Winning Wisdom
- Walking In Wisdom
- The Healing Balm
- Manifestations Of The Spirit
- Breaking The Curses Of Life
- Overcoming Forces Of Wickedness
- You Shall Not Be Barren!
- Exploring The Secrets Of Success
- Winning Prayer
- Understanding The Anointing
- Fulfilling Your Days
- Towards Mental Exploits
- Understanding Vision
- Understanding Divine Direction
- The Force Of Freedom
- Born To Win
- The Shower Of Blessing
- Riding On Prophetic Wings
- All You Need To Have All Your needs Met
- Operating In The Supernatural
- Ruling Your World
- Success in Marriage (Co-authored with Faith Oyedepo)
- The Blood Triumph
- Keys To Divine Health
- Winning Faith
- Conquering Controlling Powers
- Put Your Angels To Work
- Covenant Wealth
- Keys To Answered Prayer
- Miracle Seed
- The Hidden Covenant Of Blessing

INSIDE VIEW OF
Faith Tabernacle

Dr David Oyedepo is the Founding President of the Living Faith Church Worldwide Inc. and the Senior Pastor of the Faith Tabernacle, a 50,000 capacity sanctuary located in Canaanland, Ota, a suburb of Lagos, Nigeria.

The construction of this gigantic architectural masterpiece was completed within twelve months and dedicated on September 18, 1999, built totally debt-free and without any foreign inputs! To God alone be all the glory.

Today, Faith Tabernacle stands as the home of signs and wonders for men and women all over the world, who keep coming in droves to worship the King of kings and the Lord of lords, Jesus Christ the Son of the Living God.

OUTSIDE VIEW OF FAITH TABERNACLE

OVERVIEW OF FAITH TABERNACLE

Visit our website for more information: www.faithtabernacle.org.ng

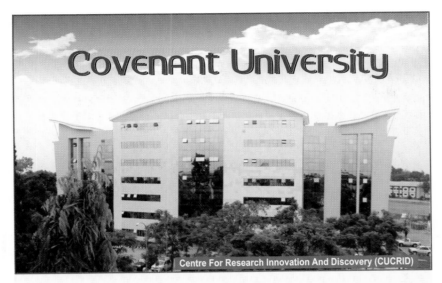

Covenant University

Centre For Research Innovation And Discovery (CUCRID)

Dr David Oyedepo is the Visioner and Chancellor of Covenant University, founded 21st October 2002. Today, Covenant University has a student population of over 6,000, all fully boarded on campus; in state of the art halls of residence. All degree programmes offered at Covenant University are fully accredited by the appropriate accrediting body. Presently, CU offers 42 degree programmes in 3 different faculties:

COLLEGE OF SCIENCE AND TECHNOLOGY:

Computer Science, Management Information System, Architecture, Building Technology, Estate Management, Industrial Mathematics, Industrial Chemistry, Industrial Physics, Biochemistry, Biology, Microbiology, Computer Engineering, Information and Communication Technology, Electrical and Electronic Engineering, Civil Engineering, Mechanical Engineering, Chemical Engineering, Petroleum Engineering.

COLLEGE OF HUMAN DEVELOPMENT:

Philosophy, Psychology, Counselling, English Language, Mass Communication, Public Relations and Advertising, Sociology and French.

COLLEGE OF BUSINESS AND SOCIAL SCIENCES:

Accounting, Taxation and Public Sector Accounting, Banking and Finance, Business Administration, Marketing, Industrial Relations and Human Resource Management, Economics, Demography and Social Statistics, International Relations, Political Science, Public Administration, Policy and Strategic Studies.

Some Facilities at Covenant University

African Leadership Development Centre

4,000-Seat University Chapel

Post Graduate Halls Of Residence

Some Facilities at Landmark University

University Library

University Chapel

Students' Hall Of Residence